SWIMMING WITH GLORY

A Spiritual Journey in the Waters of Fiji

Debby Cason

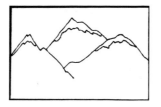

Rocky Hi Press LLC
Nathrop, Colorado

The author and publisher disclaim any responsibility or liability resulting from the actions advocated or discussed in this book.

Published by

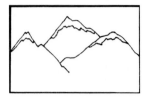

Rocky Hi Press LLC
20155 Hide Out Lane
Nathrop, Colorado 81236

SWIMMING WITH GLORY
A Spiritual Journey in the Waters of Fiji

Printed in the United States of America
First Edition
Second Printing

ISBN: 978-1-4675-3562-5

Edited by Leslie Miller, Pen For Hire
Cover design by Debby Cason and Nick Zelinger, NZ Graphics

Photo of Yellowmargin Giant Triggerfish on cover by Erwin Kodiat:
www.d-scubaclub.com
Photo of the author on back cover and with husband in Author's Bio
by Karen Campbell of Mk's Photography:
www.mksphotovideo.com

Logo by Debby Cason
Interior photographs by Debby Cason
Printed by KIMCO On Demand Printers, Denver, Colorado

DEDICATION

First of all, I dedicate this book to God within Nature, and especially within Glory, and my cat Boots.

Secondly, I dedicate this book to all human beings everywhere who are seeking to deepen and strengthen their conscious relationship with God.

Thirdly, I dedicate this book to the following Great Ones who have guided my spiritual footsteps: Jesus, the Christ; Krishna, the Christ; Paramahansa Yogananda; Mata Amritanandamayi; and the Buddha.

Last, but definitely not least, I dedicate this book to my beloved husband, Roger Cason, who is sharing the voyage of this lifetime with me and who demonstrates his spiritual stature to me every day.

FORWARD

SWIMMING WITH GLORY: A Spiritual Journey in the Waters of Fiji, is an enchanting and amazing book, all the more amazing because it's absolutely true and it awakens us to who we really are and our interconnectedness with all of God's creatures. I have known Debby Cason for many years and shared through her writings, sent from faraway lands, the nine-year journey she and her husband made on their sailboat, *Dreamer*. Their adventures were exciting to read about and to hear personally, but the story of her on-going encounters with a fish she named Glory is one of the most tender and heart-warming of all her adventures. You find yourself in the water with them as two species, both creations of a loving God, who rarely interact together, play, frolic and attune in some special mystical way in the sea. I fell in love with Glory – she isn't a fish – she's a living, intelligent manifestation of our Creator and she knows it.

Glory and Debby form a bond unheard of between people and fish. Glory plays games with her, seeks her out, hides from her and then returns. Glory obviously has a sense of humor unrecognized by most of us humans who have never taken the time to get acquainted with this part of a Greater Creation – the fish kingdom. Ultimately Glory becomes a teacher for Debby, reminding her of who she is, the many ways in which God manifests, and helps her remember Who and What are important in life.

I hated for the book to end. I became part of the family of the people on the island and began to really care about them because Debby brought them to life. I shared the Casons' adventures on their boat through the calm and rough waters. Debby's ability to create with word pictures you can see clearly in your mind makes this book a MUST READ for anyone who is ready to change paradigms and step out of the box into greater awareness.

Her experiences with Glory changed her life and mine, too. I believe the lives of all of you who read this book will also be forever changed. Never will I step into the ocean again, canoe a lake, peer down into an aquarium, without remembering that all the life in the water around me is part of the creation of a loving God – a part of me – we are ONE. Thank you Debby and Glory for helping us to remember.

Anne Puryear
Author of *STEPHEN LIVES!* and *MESSAGES FROM GOD*
Minister, therapist, writer and co-founder of
The Logos Center, Scottsdale, Arizona

ACKNOWLEDGMENTS

I am deeply grateful to Susan Donaldson, without whose generosity of spirit, Rog and I would never have been able to take our voyage in the first place. She shouldered the responsibilities of overseeing our personal paperwork during the entire nine years that we were gone without ever once complaining about the extra work it created in her already busy life. You have my eternal gratitude, Susan.

I will never forget our dear Fijian friends, Jack and Sofi Fisher, whose open hearts and genuine Fijian hospitality enriched our lives immeasurably. God willing, I hope to get back to Fiji soon to hear again Sofi's unforgettable laugh and to give that big man of hers another bear hug.

I thank Susan Tweit for getting me started on the manuscript, and also for her expertise, guidance and encouragement. I am deeply indebted to my three writing buddies in Writers Four for the successful completion of this book. There is not a shred of doubt in my mind that without the love, encouragement and editorial support of Maria Weber, Sue Greiner and Cary Unkelbach this book would never have been written. Thank you to all three of you from the bottom of my heart.

Publishing *Swimming With Glory* created its own challenges and I am extremely grateful to the following friends, without whose help I could not have succeeded in this effort: Pat Benton for always making herself available to answer my countless computer questions; Maria Weber who gave me a plethora of valuable information regarding the overall process; Leslie Miller who worked flawlessly with me to edit the manuscript; Ellen and Anthony Sanchez who helped me to understand how best to scan my photographic slides for publication; Karen Campbell who used her expertise to take professional photographs of Rog and me for the book; Chuck Gilmore who filled in with gray tone the land masses on my maps; Erwin Kodiat from Indonesia who gave me permission in the nick of time to use his true-to-life photo of a yellowmargin giant triggerfish in Bali; Nick Zelinger who completed my half-baked cover, giving it the professional look the book deserves; and I extend special gratitude to my dear husband who has played second fiddle to *Swimming With Glory* for the past three months.

Other friends who have contributed valuable suggestions and encouragement along the way are Nancy Walters, Marcy Adams, Marge Dorfmeister, Tom Rampton, Ronnie Moore, Maritza Kaniewski, and Nancy Lund of KIMCO Printing for her invaluable assistance and for working extra long hours to meet my deadline.

And finally, I am extremely grateful to the following friends who read through the manuscript before publication and praised it so highly I had no choice but to carry the project through to completion: Anne Puryear, Kathy Keidel, Rondi Smith, Shirl Holloway, Bowie Duncan, Julie Colton, Diana Edgar and Kate Neucrantz.

Debby Cason
June 19, 2012

TABLE OF CONTENTS

LOCATION OF FIJI ISLANDS

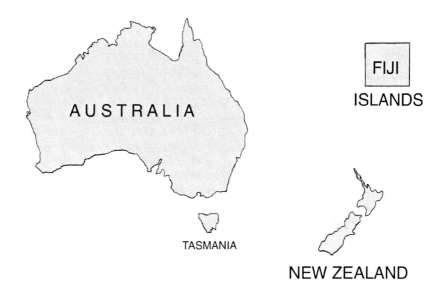

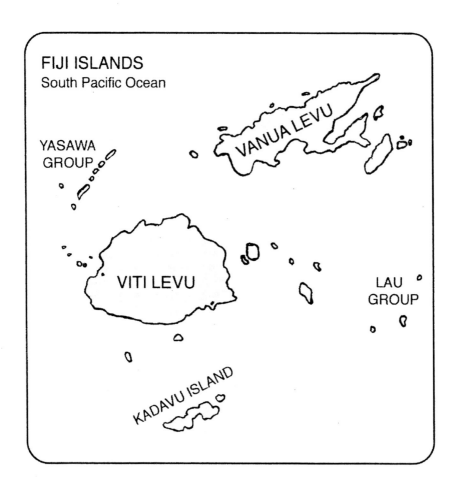

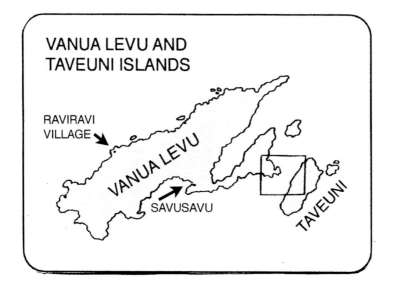

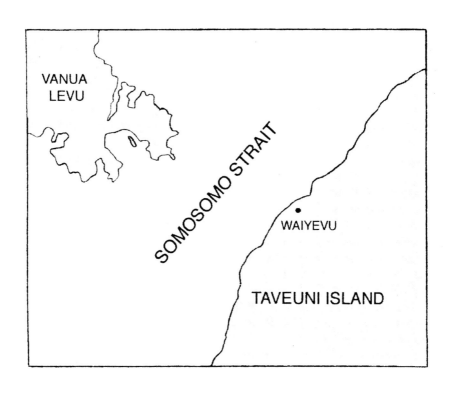

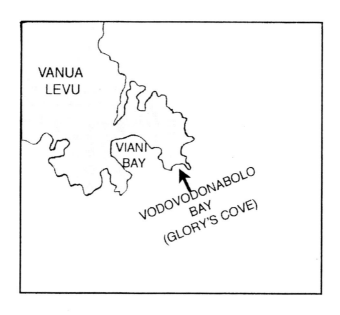

PROLOGUE

November 23, 1990

I felt fearful as I awakened at 4:00 a.m. to the sound of howling wind and the erratic motion of our forty-foot sailboat, battling the raging storm around her. Reluctantly I climbed out of our bunk, fully clothed and holding on for balance, to see how my husband, Rog, was handling the situation.

"Thank God you're here," he shouted as I opened the wooden doors separating the madness outside from our cozy home inside the boat. "I've been screaming at the top of my lungs to try to wake you up, knowing you'd never hear me up forward. We've got to reef this mainsail. It's blowing forty knots out here and the self-steering vane can't handle these conditions."

"Okay. I'm here. Do you want me to take the helm?" I asked with some trepidation, as the deafening wind accosted my ears and I saw boiling seas chasing us from the stern.

"Yes, and please hurry. I've been forced to hand steer ever since this gale hit us over two hours ago. I knew we should have reefed when I got that last weather report."

He was tired and angry. Entering the cockpit, I took stock of the situation. Our large mainsail was out as far as she could go and according to the knot meter, we were doing twelve knots over the bottom—breakneck speed for our Passport 40 sloop. This was going to be a difficult reefing job, to say the least.

"You'd better put your life vest on and harness yourself to the binnacle." Rog knew how I hated restraints, but I acquiesced to his judgment.

As Rog turned over the helm, I planted my feet far apart to absorb the motions of our ordinarily stable vessel, which was now like a bobbing cork on the high seas. Exhausted, Rog sat down on our fiberglass settee just as a breaking wave crashed into the cockpit, upsetting the delicate balance of the boat and allowing gale-force winds to strike the forward side of the sail. This recipe for disaster sent the boom flying over our heads to the other side of the boat in a millisecond.

"Oh my God!" I saw that the traveler on our stern had pulled out of the deck, allowing the end of the boom to fly forward. All the pressure of the heavy aluminum boom was now concentrated on the leeward shroud.

"Head her up," Rog yelled. "I've got to get this sail down!" As he stood up to work his way forward, we saw that in addition to loosing our traveler, the flying jibe had also broken our gooseneck, the fitting that holds the forward end of the boom to the mast. We were seriously disabled and in a dangerous situation.

We had to get our mainsail down immediately so we didn't lose our entire rig. Doing it was going to require all of the agility and strength Roger possessed. I felt terrible for having put us into this precarious predicament. I had voted for furling up the genoa but not reefing the mainsail six hours earlier, when we learned a winter storm off the coast of Oregon was moving rapidly down the California coast and was likely to hit us before we reached San Diego.

Regardless of my remorse, I had to concentrate upon the job at hand. Heading our boat, *Dreamer*, up into a close reach so Rog could pull down the mainsail would put us temporarily sideways to the onrushing swells. More water cascaded into our cockpit and I prayed that God would protect Rog as he slowly worked his way up toward the mast, unhooking and re-hooking his safety harness onto the lifeline as he simultaneously grabbed onto the handrail bolted through our cabin top.

"*Where is that light coming from?*" I wondered as a spotlight suddenly blinded me. "*There must be another vessel out here! All we need now is trying to avoid a collision while maneuvering our disabled boat."* Scary thoughts filled my mind as I tried to judge how far away the other boat was from us. It seemed so close! *"With a spotlight like that, it must be a fishing boat,"* I thought. *"I hope we don't get tangled up in any nets, and above all, I hope we don't accidentally crash into each other!"*

My attention was brought back to Rog who was yelling, "Release the halyard."

As the gale blew my words back over our stern, I doubted he could hear me, but nonetheless I yelled back, "Roger, Roger." Ordinarily, I would release the main halyard gradually, but I now gave it a lot of slack. The pressure of the wind in our large sail would hinder the gravity that ordinarily pulled the sail down easily. In addition to exerting as much force as he could to pull down the sail, Rog also had to hold onto the mast steps as tightly as possible. Essentially, he was now standing on what had become the bucking bronco of our foredeck.

Our boom was banging back and forth and the sail was flailing mercilessly, adding to the cacophony of the storm. Despite the vexing spotlight from the other vessel, we were unable to ascertain whether any serious damage was being done to our rig. This was a major concern.

It was torturous watching Rog claw down that sail while holding on for dear life, when I could do nothing to assist him except stand behind the wheel and try to help *Dreamer* take each wave as gently as possible. I was grateful that nothing was ending up in the ocean, including Rog!

4

The bright light was dead ahead of us now, making it impossible to see the shape of the other vessel. As soon as the sail was completely down and Rog came back into the cockpit, I urged him, "Please go check the radar screen and find out how far away that other vessel is before you do anything else."

In a few minutes he relieved my anxiety. "It's two nautical miles away."

"Which way is it going, can you tell?"

"It looks like it's bobbing around, just like us."

We knew it wasn't a tanker or any other commercial vessel because they have specific, identifiable lights. By studying these light configurations, it's possible to determine in which direction the vessel is traveling.

"I guess we're safe right now." I held our course just off the wind as Rog grabbed a handful of sail ties, six-foot long nylon straps that are about an inch wide. He proceeded to go forward again, and working his way from the forward end of the boom to the aft end, he was able to tie the sail to the boom at about four-foot intervals. As soon as Rog returned to the cockpit, I headed *Dreamer* south again, away from the eerie spotlight that had worried me throughout this ordeal.

"Rog, I'm so sorry," I said.

"It's all right. Shit happens. It wasn't your fault. We have to wait until first light to see if the rig is okay. In the meantime, we have a broken traveler and a broken gooseneck. If nothing else, this storm has enabled us to learn about *Dreamer's* weaknesses. We're going to have to check the mainsail for tears, too. By the way, it feels like we're soaring down these swells. How fast are we going?"

I checked the knot meter. "Six knots," I replied.

"That's unbelievable. We don't have a single sail up and yet we're doing six knots. I wonder if these waves are going to be breaking across the San Diego Harbor entrance."

"I don't know," I said, "but we can call the Coast Guard to find out."

"Good idea. Let's wait until we get a little bit closer. I just need to space out for a while."

We fell into silence and it wasn't long before Roger's head began to nod. About an hour later, the light of pre-dawn began to break over the stormy seas. I ran my eyes up and down our shrouds and detected no damage to the standing rigging, the thick wires that support and hold the mast in an upright position.

"How are we doing?" Roger's query interrupted my inspection.

"Just fine. It's now about 6:00 and the wind shows no signs of abating. Do you feel rested enough to call the Coast Guard about the harbor entrance? I think getting into the harbor will be our last challenge. Hopefully we won't have any problems starting up the engine."

Rog picked up the cockpit mike. "U.S. Coast Guard out of San Diego, this is the sailing vessel *Dreamer*. Do you copy?"

"*Dreamer*, this is the Coast Guard. How can we help you? Over."

"U.S. Coast Guard, we are approaching San Diego from the north. We have sustained damage to our sailboat in the gale and are surfing down the swells toward you under bare poles at a speed of six knots. We should reach the harbor entrance in about one hour and we are concerned about the sea conditions there. Are the waves breaking across the entrance? Over."

"*Dreamer*, this is the Coast Guard. We copy you but cannot relay the requested information. Over."

"U.S. Coast Guard, this is *Dreamer*. Why can't you provide us with information about the conditions at the entrance to San Diego Harbor? This is a safety issue. Over."

"*Dreamer*, this is the Coast Guard. We repeat that we cannot provide you with the requested information. Over."

"This is *Dreamer*, clear with the Coast Guard and standing by."

I could sense the storm clouds brewing across Roger's countenance. "What do you suppose that was all about?" I asked.

"They're probably afraid of getting sued. The Coast Guard used to be so helpful only a few years ago. Remember when I told you about the Newport 30 sailboat, *Harry*, that I was helping race down the coast? We were in big seas, beam on at night, about twenty-five miles off the coast of Santa Cruz. One of the co-owners, Dick, smashed his head open on the radio direction finder when a particularly large swell struck *Harry* broadside.

Blood was gushing from the gash in Dick's forehead and I couldn't stop the bleeding. After about fifteen minutes, Dick asked me to call the Coast Guard.

"In response to our emergency call, they deployed a helicopter, hoisted Dick off in a basket they lowered to the deck and whisked him off to the nearest medical facility."

"That's amazing, Rog. As you describe it, that experience was almost the exact opposite from the Coast Guard's response to our current situation."

"*Dreamer, Dreamer*, this is the sailing vessel *Geronimo*. Come in, *Dreamer*."

Rog picked up the cockpit mike, responding to the call, "*Geronimo, Geronimo*, this is *Dreamer*. Over."

"*Dreamer*, we just copied your conversation with the Coast Guard and are calling to assure you conditions at San Diego Harbor are manageable. We cleared that entrance ourselves about a half hour ago. Over."

"Sailing vessel *Geronimo*, this is *Dreamer*. Thank you for your information. We are deeply appreciative. Over."

"You're welcome, *Dreamer*. *Geronimo* clear."

"*Dreamer* clear."

"Boy, that's a relief," I said.

"I'll say," Rog replied.

The next forty minutes passed quickly and with the help of the early morning light, our entrance into San Diego proved uneventful. It took another forty minutes to power all the way down the bay to the Chula Vista Marina where we found our prearranged berth and tied up. We would worry about checking in later. Exhausted, we hit the bunk as soon as possible.

One last thought crossed my mind: that strange spotlight out at sea on a stormy night reminded me of the light of a loving God that was always watching over us, and would likely continue doing so during our upcoming voyage through the South Pacific, with all its inevitable challenges. I felt peaceful as I drifted off into a deep sleep.

Chapter 1

PARADISE FOUND

I sat in the bosun's chair, three stories above the surface of the azure sea. The water lapped gently over the multicolored reefs, the soft corals swaying in splendid roses and golds, peaches and violets.

"It's just beyond the next reef," my husband bellowed from the cockpit below me.

"No, no, no," I shouted back down. "I want to anchor here, in this gorgeous cove to starboard. Look, nobody lives there. We can explore Viani Bay next week. No one's expecting us and we have all the time in the world."

We had just navigated through the beautiful but dangerous Rainbow Reef of Somosomo Strait, between Taveuni and Vanua Levu Islands in northeastern Fiji.

"Come on down," Rog yelled, "so I can check the charts."

I scrambled down to the deck, unhooking the halyard from the bosun's chair and refastening it into its ring on the mast. Entering the cockpit of our Passport 40 sailboat, I took the wheel, setting our course in a circular motion not unlike a dog chasing its tail, while Rog studied charts of the cove.

The date was September 4, 1995. My husband and I had decided to spend the upcoming five-month cyclone season in Fiji aboard our sailing yacht *Dreamer*, instead of returning to New Zealand for a fourth time. This would give us time to kick back and explore, as well as more thoroughly delve into the lives of the Fijian people we had come to love. Although we had no way of knowing it, the treasure we were about to discover would add a richness and depth of experience to our voyage that would make the risk worthwhile indeed.

"Well," Rog said finally, "the cove looks safe enough, but there are a few bommies toward the center. I'd like you to go back up the mast while we anchor."

Bommies were our nickname for the coral heads underneath the surface of the water. They're wonderful for snorkeling and diving purposes but you certainly wouldn't want to hit one with your boat, since they have the consistency of concrete. I headed back up the mast as Rog turned *Dreamer* into the cove. From my vantage point, I could see those interesting bommies as well as a pristine, snow-white beach lined with swaying coconut palms.

"Let's take her about fifty yards to starboard," I called down. "That will keep our nose into the wind, and we should drift right back to about where we are now once the anchor is set."

Once in position, I again scrambled down from my perch and hurried to the cockpit to take over the wheel. Rog went forward onto the bow to release the anchor, which made its distinctive rattling sound as it plummeted in controlled motion to the white sand thirty feet below. The water was so clear we could easily see the anchor flukes grabbing into the white crystals of coral sand as I gently backed *Dreamer*. Once I felt that slight tug, I kept her in reverse for another half minute to assure the set of the anchor, before returning the gear to neutral and shutting down the engine.

We were home; for how long, we knew not.

A moment later I caught sight of a splash of orange-pink color moving about in the water off our port quarter. "Rog, come and look at this fish. I think she wants to swim with me!"

"Honey, you've been reading too many fantasies."

Although to this day I cannot explain why, my intuition insisted that I ease myself quietly down our swim ladder to interact with this inquisitive Pisces. It's possible that my impulse arose from reading a Peter Benchley novel, *The Girl of the Sea of Cortez*, in which the heroine, a native Mexican girl, befriends a manta ray. The book relates her struggle to save the fish population from villagers who planned to dynamite the reef where the manta ray lived. I loved that book and related to the heroine so strongly, I sometimes felt like I *was* that Mexican girl, swimming with the fishes I loved.

I eased my way down the ladder with my mask and snorkel on. Holding myself below the surface of the water by grasping the foot of the ladder, I found myself face to face with what I later learned was a yellowmargin triggerfish, one of two types of giant triggerfish. Easily the length of my arm from elbow to fingertips, giant triggerfish get their name from a dorsal fin that usually lies flat against the top of their bodies. Fear or danger triggers this fin to stand up straight, enabling the fish to wedge itself into a hole or crevice as a defense against predators. In addition, triggerfish have formidable teeth designed for chomping away at coral, and if provoked, they can deliver a nasty bite.

This particular giant triggerfish hovered about twelve feet away, looking right at me. Feelings of elation overwhelmed me as we remained face to face for that first encounter together. I immediately named her Glory for the glory of God in all creation. In my mind, she was a reflection of Mother Nature, the divine feminine.

I slowly turned away from her. Ever so gently, without making a splash, I swam quietly away, fully expecting that she would follow me, even as the manta ray swam with Peter Benchley's heroine. But when I turned around, the fish was nowhere in sight. Greatly disappointed, I held onto the hope that she would reappear sometime during our stay in Vodovodonabolo Bay.

Our first evening passed in heavenly solitude and gratitude for our surroundings. We enjoyed mashed potatoes and salad on our teak, drop-leaf cockpit table, while listening to the gentle lapping of the incoming tide on the shore and observing the buildup of gentle cumulous clouds that would later provide a splendid sunset. I thought about the brave little fish, hoping one day I'd see her again.

It was my habit to arise at the crack of dawn and head to the bow for forty minutes of yoga-like energization exercises, followed by another forty minutes or so of meditation. I cannot adequately describe the joy and serenity this custom brought me. When I first began meditating my restlessness was acute and my body rebelled with intense neck and shoulder pain, but that discomfort had dissolved with the passage of time and the tenacity of the commitment I had made while studying the teachings of Paramahansa Yogananda.

The energization exercises are meant to be done with eyes closed, to concentrate upon the energy entering and flowing through various body parts. I found this to be near impossible when practicing on the bow of a boat in utopia. Beauty assailed my senses. The smell of the frangipani blossoms wafting from shore, along with the perfect hues of blue, green and white, kept me spellbound as I performed the challenging postures of the series. By the time I finished, my body hummed like a bumblebee serenely buzzing from flower to flower. My heart swelled with gratitude and I easily slipped into that altered state of quietude, sensing the presence of God everywhere, within and without.

One of our favorite breakfasts followed my dip into divinity — banana sourdough pancakes. Yummy! We contemplated our day. "Rog, would you swim ashore with me to check this place out? I think I could lie on that beach for hours without any problem at all."

"You know," he said, "You've been waking me up every night for the past five nights with your coughing. I really think you should stay out of the water for a few days until your body clears up that cough. We could take *Gos* in, though, if you'd like." Rog and I had a way of nicknaming everything. We called our ten-foot, gray rubber inflatable dinghy *Gos* because it reminded us of a baby duckling following its mother, while trailing behind *Dreamer.*

Reaching the shore, we discovered no trace of human life. I was amazed. Why wouldn't someone want to live in this splendid cove? The fact that no one was there heightened our enjoyment of this heaven on earth. Although we knew of two other sailing vessels in northeastern Fiji, we decided to keep Vodovodonabolo Bay our secret for as long as we possibly could.

After checking out the flora, we settled in on our towels and Rog quickly fell asleep. I continued reading until I got too hot. Easing into the pristine water to cool off, I thought about the yellowmargin giant triggerfish and sighed, realizing I had not seen her again.

Then, both concerned for Roger's delicate skin and cognizant of his suggestion that I stay out of the water, I woke him up and we proceeded to stroll leisurely along the shore to the far side of the bay. Warm and cozy, we snuggled up on the sandbar atop our largest beach towel, safe under the shade of a majestic palm. Eventually, our legs entwined and we were lost in a sea of lovemaking. By the time we regained consciousness of the world around us, we found that the sun was ever so slowly declining in the western sky.

"Here's to another shitty day in paradise," Rog joked, sealing our passion with a kiss.

Back aboard *Dreamer*, I prepared our dinner—fresh, ripe pawpaw picked on the shore, filled with tuna salad. We never found out why the natives referred to papaya as pawpaw. Perhaps it was an easier English translation for them. But that reminded me of Viani Bay, just around the tip of this bay. We had anchored in Viani Bay for over two weeks the year before, and found the inhabitants to be the most congenial Fijians we had met thus far. We assumed they didn't know we were so close and yet so far away.

"Rog, how long do you think we should stay here? Now that we have acquired our permit to spend the cyclone season in Fiji, I don't think we have to be in any great hurry. What do you think?"

"Mañana," he replied, indicating he was in no big hurry either. I was glad.

The very next morning, as I headed to the bow for my morning routine, I noticed that distinctive orange-pink color nearing the surface of the water. My heart leapt for joy!

Undaunted by human presence, my brave little adventurer began swimming around *Dreamer's* perimeter. I noticed she had a peculiar way of tilting her body so that she could look up at me whenever she paused in her circumambulation.

I marveled as I soaked in her majesty. Glory was about fifteen inches long and about eight inches tall. She was thick for a fish, measuring about two inches in depth. Her distinctive coloration—orange-pink, golden-yellow and tropical blue-green—matched by her boldness in approaching a vessel whose inhabitants could easily cause her demise, took my breath away. Although Rog and I were not avid fisher people, the Fijians delight in the flesh of giant triggerfish, which are targeted frequently by spear fishermen.

I decided to delay my morning routine long enough to sketch Glory as well as I could from my vantage point three feet above the water. Looking closely, I saw that the orange-pink color that originally caught my eye was confined to the area around her mouth, which I called her beak, for lack of a better word. The bold golden-yellow stripe that was the source of her common name outlined Glory's dorsal, anal and caudal fins, and was emphasized by an adjacent stripe of black. Blue-green diamonds covered the vast majority of her body, and her pectoral fin was pale blue. Her eyes were vividly green, bulging out from each side of her head. Four black lines accentuated her eyes like make-up, with two lines behind and two lines underneath each eye.

Our book, *Micronesian Reef Fishes*, told me Glory's scientific name was Pseudobalistes Flavimarginatus.

Using the small blue pectoral fins on either side of her body, she was able to remain almost stationary in the water as she gazed up at me from time to time. Suddenly I remembered watching Loi Fisher, a twelve-year-old Fijian girl from Viani Bay, feeding a wild fish with chunks of the bread Rog occasionally baked. While I knew bread wasn't necessary to maintain our already electric relationship, I wanted to give something back to Glory. I quietly went below, extracted some bread from one of the hanging food nets in the main salon, and returned to the cockpit. Glory was waiting for me in the water just off the stern of the boat.

I was thrilled with this little fish, so grateful that this manifestation of God was for some reason romancing me. Feeding Glory, I was impressed with her large, white teeth and strong jaws. I later learned that in addition to chomping on coral, triggerfish use their teeth and jaws to eat the giant clams that are prevalent in Fiji.

Several days passed in this way. Glory came up to the surface every morning during my meditation time and again around 5:00 each evening. I felt we were communing telepathically, otherwise why would she return twice a day to visit with me? Ours was a communication of love, awe, and respect. Perhaps her interest in me was based more on curiosity than on love but I definitely felt a very special, magnetic energy between us.

Although Rog rarely witnessed our morning reveries, when Glory came back in the early evenings, he also drank in her splendor and received the miracle of her involvement with us. I *never* wanted to leave Vodovodonabolo Bay.

Chapter 2

SHAKY BEGINNINGS

What started as a sore throat and midnight coughing spells evolved into something worse. For the next two days I stayed in the bunk as my body struggled to heal from flu, with fever, vomiting, and diarrhea. We were our own medical team on board *Dreamer*. In this case, our most effective tools were extra blankets and lots of water to flush and sweat out the fever and flu. As I rolled groggily in and out of sleep, I found myself reviewing my life and what had brought me to this point in time and space.

When I was quite young, between the ages of six and eight, I distinctly remember three experiences. The first involved a question I posed to my unsuspecting mother after she'd had a miscarriage. "Mom, what would happen to me if I were never born?"

"Well," she began, "you simply would never be."

"But that's impossible. I could never not be." My young mind was clear about that. My mother had no further response to my insistent questions, suggesting that I go out to play and forget about it. But I never did forget about it.

The second experience occurred in a locker room where I was changing from street clothes into a bathing suit, before going swimming in a public pool. There was no one but me in the locker room and suddenly I felt extremely alone. I was struck by how very strange it felt to exist in a human body.

The third experience occurred several times during the spring and fall. Flocks of migrating birds landed daily in a huge weeping willow tree located about half a block from our home. Raucous chatter filled the air with the sense of these birds' freedom and joy. During the early evenings, I sat on the curb across the street from this tree, but instead of identifying with the birds' freedom and joy, I felt melancholy because I was encased in a human body: earthbound, trapped, unable to fly through the skies as they did.

When I was eight, a friend with whom I walked to and from school, rode bikes and played in a tree shack was suddenly struck by a car and killed. Once again, I felt terribly alone and tried to process his departure from the planet. I tried to imagine him in heaven and what that would be like. Would I ever see him again? I must say that these experiences made a lasting impression on me.

I was fortunate to have been raised in an upper middle class family. My father, a self-made man, invested wisely over the years, enabling our family to own a summer home on Shelter Island, New York. We were members of the Shelter Island Yacht Club, where I learned how to sail and race, starting when I was ten. Sailing gave me that feeling of freedom, a love for the water, and a feeling of connectedness with Nature.

During my teenage years when I began to date, my father's alcoholism escalated significantly. He couldn't seem to handle my dating and flew into rages almost every night during dinner. The family learned to lay low when Dad was around, cherishing the serenity in our home whenever he was gone on one of his two-week sales trips.

After graduating from junior college in New Jersey and Katharine Gibbs Secretarial School in New York City, I married a native Shelter Islander, a young man who was dearly loved by the year-round residents. Together we built a small marina on his family property, harvesting scallops in the fall and working on private yachts in West Palm Beach, Florida in the winter. Although I also loved him dearly, the marriage failed after three years due to excessive alcohol consumption on both of our parts. I walked out because we were in a downward spiral. My alcoholism warped my sense of reality, and I felt lonely even in the midst of many friends and loved ones. I was grateful I had no children, because I might have caused them great psychological harm.

After the divorce, I returned to "The Big Apple," eventually becoming a registered representative with the New York Stock Exchange. I had a great time in New York, making lots of friends, dating, joining group houses in the Hamptons during the summers and in Vermont during the winters. I got involved with Don, a man who loved life and managed to keep my self-esteem in good shape, despite my daily drinking.

Yet one day I just up and left this wonderful person and moved to California, where I met Rog. Sadly, alcohol made me an emotional basket case, regardless of what my external life looked like. I had a great job in San Francisco as executive secretary to the Chairman of the Board of a title insurance company. Rog was a successful CPA with a reputable company. Together we skied in the Sierras and sailed on San Francisco Bay. What could be better? But no matter what I did or where I moved, I couldn't escape the emptiness inside me.

Eight months later, Roger's firm asked him to transfer to its New York office, and he asked me to marry him. This sent me into a tailspin because I was unable to say yes or no. I respected Rog but missed the easy-going, deep friendship I'd had with Don. My confusion was such that I never really said yes to Rog, instead allowing Spirit to carry me all the way back to New York until one day I found myself at the altar. To this day, thirty-six years later, Rog still calls me his reluctant bride.

The first year of our marriage was, without a doubt, the worst year of my life. My emotional upheavals were gargantuan. At one point early on, I seriously considered getting the marriage annulled. This idea reduced my thirty-eight-year-old husband to tears, the first and last time I ever saw him cry. As a result, I started thinking about the havoc I was wreaking in other people's lives with my erratic behavior. Soon thereafter I joined Alcoholics Anonymous.

My first year of the program was extremely difficult. I could no longer numb the deep emotional scars left in my psyche from my parents' alcoholism. I cried daily, desperate to run away, but my sponsor told me over and over again, "No major changes for one year." I was stuck.

The saving grace was reconnecting with my strong childhood faith in God. I might not have been happy but I was excited about this renewed attunement and began reading all types of inspirational literature, starting with Emmet Fox's books. After a year of sobriety, I read *Autobiography Of A Yogi* by Paramahansa Yogananda, which gave me a huge "ah-ha" experience. As I devoured page after page, I suddenly understood how the entire cosmos works. I understood the totality of Jesus' teachings and ministry. Everything made sense.

I was enthralled by Yogananda's detailed descriptions of the higher states of consciousness, achievable through daily meditation, and I resolutely committed myself to the life-long practice of Kriya Yoga, taught in his Self-Realization Fellowship Lessons. I was transformed from a person seeking happiness in the external world to a person seeking happiness from within.

One of the many audiocassettes I purchased from Self-Realization Fellowship was entitled, "Understanding the Soul's Need for God." In that talk, Sri Daya Mata explained that the reason a person turns to alcohol is to fulfill a deep yearning for the natural blissful state of the soul. However, the alcohol gives only a false, temporary feeling of bliss which eventually backfires. That certainly was my experience.

While my outer life seemed to have stabilized, my hunger for a deep and continuous conscious contact with God kept me dissatisfied. In the spring of 1986, Roger's firm asked whether he would be willing to return to San Francisco to run the audit department. Roger's love for the Bay Area won over the more practical aspects of his upwardly mobile career path in New York City.

By May of '86 we were back in San Francisco, in a beautifully renovated building originally constructed in 1908, just after the famous San Francisco earthquake and fire of 1906. Our new home included an eight-foot skylight in the ceiling at the top of our thirty-eight stairs, beamed ceilings, mahogany woodwork, original wooden floors, two fireplaces, and floor-to-ceiling windows in our newly renovated great room. Our deck overlooked San Francisco Bay, with of a view from Angel Island and Alcatraz past Mt. Tamalpais, the Marin Headlands and the Golden Gate Bridge, all the way around to the Marina

District and on over to Russian Hill. We were situated near the corner of Jackson and Hyde where the cable cars traveling from Fisherman's Wharf to Union Square and back made a ninety degree turn, clanging their delightful bells about once an hour. Was this not perfection?

But just one year later, mergers and a host of other circumstances at Rog's firm caused a conflict of interest, requiring either that we leave the San Francisco area, or that Rog leave the firm he had given twenty-five years of dedicated service.

We debated for about one week, knowing in our hearts we had no desire to leave our beautiful condominium with its unique charm. After our move back to San Francisco, we had purchased a beautiful Passport 40 sloop-rigged sailboat with a twelve-foot, eight-inch beam. Her prior owner called her *Indulgence*, but we renamed her *Dreamer*. She had a gorgeous teak interior with an easy to maintain fiberglass hull, highlighted with teak trim on the exterior, especially in the roomy aft cockpit. *Dreamer* was a blue-water boat, capable of crossing oceans. We began dreaming of sailing to foreign lands. We reasoned that we were both young and strong enough to handle rough weather on the open ocean now, but if we waited until retirement age, it could be too late in our lives to undertake a strenuous voyage. So, Rog officially retired on December 31, 1987, at the ripe old age of forty-nine. I was forty-one.

While exciting in some ways, the ensuing three years were not easy. I was accustomed to having freedom to choose my own schedule, attend AA meetings and share my emotions and experiences on deep levels with trusted friends. Once Rog retired, he wanted me to be involved in every trip he took to the Schoonmacher Marina in Sausalito, while preparing *Dreamer* for our voyage. Slowly, I watched my normal life and deep friendships ebb away.

In the meantime, Rog was still drinking. Although he never exhibited the daily rages my alcoholic father flew into, instead he retired into silence like my mother had done. Once Rog picked up that first drink around cocktail hour, he became absorbed in reading or busied himself tinkering around on the computer until he went to sleep. There was little inter-personal communication between us.

I don't think I ever consciously knew just how lonely I felt during this time. I knew that I never felt heard by Rog and I missed the deeper connections with my close girlfriends. Finally, during a thirteen-day rafting trip down the Grand Canyon in May of 1988, I accepted a gin and tonic offered to me by one of the rafting guides. I was soon drinking again—twelve years of sobriety washed down the drain.

Now at least I could sit and drink with Rog in the evenings, although our sharing was always on a superficial level, about the boat or world affairs or the weather. I didn't know how to break into a deeper level of communication with Rog. After being raised by an alcoholic father who raged at me and the rest of my family every night from the age of fourteen, I was too scared to be vulnerable with another alcoholic male. It was easier to just drink with my husband and avoid any attempt at real intimacy.

On the surface though, Rog and I worked well together, outfitting *Dreamer* just the way we wanted her for long passages. There was so much to be done: ordering new sails; changing the standing rigging and adding a roller furler for the genoa; ordering and installing a self-steering vane to the stern; installing solar panels and wind generators to supplement the power generated by running our diesel engine; installing an inverter so that we could use 110 watt appliances on board; installing and learning to use a weather fax, a single side band radio, electronic self-steering and an EPIRB (emergency position-indicating radio beacon); purchasing and installing a life raft, and a heating unit to keep the cabin warm should we find ourselves in cold weather. The list went on and on, and included selling our condominium in San Francisco. We finally found ourselves ready to leave Sausalito on Thanksgiving of 1990.

After experiencing the severe storm sailing down the California coast that Thanksgiving Day weekend, we knew we had more work to do. While we were repairing and improving *Dreamer*, we also began repairing and rebuilding both our individual lives and our relationship within the meeting rooms of Alcoholics Anonymous. Rog and I expressed our anger and disappointments with one another. We were never met with judgment or criticism from the group. Instead, we were continually given encouragement and love until we finally learned to love each other and ourselves.

The tenet, "No major changes for one year," kept us in San Diego for seventeen months, staying sober, going to meetings, working the twelve steps, and making behavioral changes. We also learned Morse code to acquire our ham radio licenses and after building up layers of varnish on our exterior cap rails and hand rails, I applied a bright yellow, marine epoxy paint to avoid the necessity of constantly varnishing in the tropics.

By the time we were ready to leave the USA on April 22, 1992 for our 2,700 mile passage across the Pacific, we were able to tell friends that in addition to the thrill of the sailing adventure, our goal was to spread light and love wherever we went.

During that first long passage from San Diego to the Marquesas Islands of French Polynesia, we were out of sight of land for twenty-seven days. This will always remain in my heart as one of the highlights of my life. My world consisted of Rog, *Dreamer*, God and myself. Spirit was obvious everywhere—in the wind, in the rain, in the squalls, in the sunshine and blue sky, in the stars, in the waves, in the vast blue ocean, and within each other and our boat. I thrived in the solitude of this wholly spiritual environment. I hoped it would never end.

As we approached landfall on Hiva Oa Island, I became irritable. Rog commented that my attitude was ruining the completion of our passage. "But I don't want to make landfall. Can't we just stay out here on the ocean?

We have enough food and water." This conversation occurred after seven straight days of squally weather when almost all the other wives, I learned later, were dying to get off of their boats. But I felt so close to Spirit, I didn't care about the weather. I just wanted to remain in the embrace of the Cosmic Beloved.

However, we did make our landfall. Rog and I met and enjoyed the locals wherever we went, exchanging pens, colored pencils and crayons, notebooks and coloring books, T-shirts and audio cassette tapes, all in exchange for fresh fruits and vegetables. The gifts we most enjoyed giving to the natives were Polaroid photos of themselves and beach balls of planet Earth as seen from our satellites, without any political boundaries. They loved these gifts and this helped us to make friends with people wherever we went. I also brought my guitar ashore from time to time and sang songs, especially to the school children. Occasionally I would even see a fisherman in his dugout stand up and dance to the beat of my song.

We attended church services in languages we didn't understand, but the lovely a cappella harmonies of their devotional songs were easily understood. After church, we were frequently invited to our new friends' homes for their noontime Sunday meal, the biggest meal of their week. In exchange, we often invited families on board *Dreamer* for meals, videos, diving and/or fishing expeditions and singing. We had medical supplies on board and could help with simple problems, such as the skin sores that seemed to be their most prevalent ailment.

With our modern-day supplies, we were sometimes able to help with boat and engine repairs; at other times, it was the locals who helped us.

Every morning I did all or at least part of my forty-minute exercise routine, followed by a minimum of another forty minutes of meditation and often much longer. My life seemed to be headed in the right direction and I felt happy. I was as yet unaware of a deep sadness that remained hidden, until one glorious day in the Tuamotus Atolls of French Polynesia. It was July 7, 1992, a sublime day in an incredible environment. I sat in the bosun's chair high above the water, looking for coral heads below the surface. Roger was at the wheel listening for my directions as we navigated across the gorgeous lagoon, from just inside of Passe Garue to the windward side of Raroia Atoll. The scene was just like a postcard: deep blue sky and clear blue water with white beaches and swaying coconut palms on the distant shore.

Here I was in a tropical paradise with a loving husband, fulfilling our dream of sailing the South Seas and yet tears were rolling down my cheeks, unbeknownst to Roger, thank God. I was still sad. I was still empty inside despite sixteen years of a happy marriage to a good husband, fifteen years of prayer and meditation, and all of the material blessings one could want. I had gone through a thorough inner cleansing from years of introspection, writing and sharing in Alcoholics Anonymous. So what was the problem? I yearned with all my heart for Oneness with the Divine. My heart hurt in its aching for that fulfillment. I was slowly giving up hope of ever finding that one true and lasting inner happiness.

September, 1995, more than three years later, we began our second season in beautiful Fiji. These few days of reflection while recovering from the flu gave me the opportunity to see that my life was good, very good in fact. Yes, I'd had the usual bumps along the road. As my neighbor in New York once said, "Everybody has his story." We've all had conflict, joys, successes, failures. Thinking about these last three years during which we continually experienced the awesome beauty of Nature and the friendship of people from other cultures, I realized I hadn't had another bitterly sad experience like the one in the Tuamotus. My overall level of joy was ever-increasing.

But I also realized that I had dedicated my life to the total merging of my individual spirit or consciousness with that of my Creator. Until that happened, I knew that I would retain a sense of sadness deep within myself, usually hidden, but there nevertheless.

This feeling of longing for Divine connection was portrayed beautifully in one of the original Star Trek episodes. A lost starship was transmitting plaintive signals throughout space, seeking the attention and the return of its creator. After the Enterprise came to the rescue, there followed a beautiful merging ceremony. One Enterprise crewman, representing the lost ship's creator, merged his physical being with a human form materialized from the composite energy remaining in the lost starship. The two human forms merged together in a tube. During the merging, their atoms of life force integrated in a dazzling display denoting love, union and bliss.

My hat goes off to the insightful Gene Roddenberry, the creator and producer of the original Star Trek. He was a visionary, a true metaphysician. The immense popularity of Star Trek gives me hope that mankind is on the brink of readiness for whatever lies ahead of it, as I was on the brink of readiness for what lay ahead of me.

Chapter 3

SWIMMING WITH GLORY

A week later, I had recovered from the flu and felt well enough to be back on deck. It was a still, perfect morning: temperature just right as always, sky an unfettered blue. I realized I hadn't had a coughing fit in two nights. It was about 6:30 a.m. and there at the stern was my faithful friend, Glory. Perhaps it was time for me to try swimming with her again.

Wearing a bathing suit, mask and snorkel, I once again quietly lowered myself down the ladder and eased into the water, facing the direction where I last saw Glory from the cockpit. As my head submerged, there she was-- a bit closer this time at about nine feet away--and looking straight into my eyes. With deep respect and appreciation, we gazed at each other calmly for about half a minute before I turned my body a hundred and eighty degrees and ever so quietly swam away from her for about a boat length. Sure enough, this time when I stopped and turned around, I found that she had followed me. We were now face-to-face, about six feet apart, with Glory three feet below me. Suddenly she did an about-face and began gently swimming away from me. *"Follow her, follow her,"* my inner voice screamed. *"This is what you've been waiting for!"*

Somehow, Glory's spatial cognition enabled her to swim at the exact same speed I maintained swimming silently behind her without flippers, relying on the breast stroke and the frog kick. I was snorkeling on the surface, and she was at the perfect distance ahead and below me so that I could see her constantly through my goggles. We swam toward the western side of the bay and continued in this direction until the bottom began to rise up, forming the edge of the bay. Glory turned ninety degrees to the left, heading for the outer reaches of the bay and I gladly followed. Suddenly, about nine feet below the surface, I saw a fish that looked exactly like Glory. I shouted telepathically, *"Glory, I see him! Thank you so much for introducing me to your mate."* As soon as my transmission was complete, Glory made another left hand turn and led me right back to the foot of *Dreamer's* ladder.

I felt like I had died and gone to heaven. My gratitude toward the Almighty knew no bounds. Glory hovered at the stern of the boat; I wanted to swim over and give her a great big hug, but of course I knew I couldn't do that. The only way I knew to thank her for this amazing adventure was to climb up the ladder and reward her with some bread and that's exactly what I did. I was bursting with a feeling I could hardly contain, a joy in my heart that no words can adequately describe. This was truly a state of bliss.

The next day Glory was again awaiting my arrival on deck. I decided to stretch my luck and eased into the water. This time, Glory swam over to me right away. She did a little acknowledgment dance, quivering ever so slightly in anticipation, then she led me to a deep coral head upon which she descended. I tried to follow her down but without flippers I couldn't make it more than about ten feet before I had to resurface. I looked around for her but she must have scooted through a hole in the bommie.

I started to swim around *Dreamer*, the way Glory does, and before I was all the way around she rejoined me. We swam together for about five more minutes but without a particular destination like we had yesterday. Then she led me over to *her* bommie, swam down twelve feet to the top of it and began chomping at the coral. Little puffs of coral dust filtered into the water as I watched Glory actually eating coral. Knowing the hardness of this substance, I was more than impressed by the strength of her jaws and teeth. Soon Glory swam back to me and led me home to *Dreamer*, signifying that our swim together was over. We'd been in the water together for twenty minutes, ten fewer than yesterday.

That afternoon I fell into a reverie about Glory. I couldn't believe that she was hanging out with me just for bread. I felt strongly that there was something much greater at work here, something that involved my constant, conscious search for God during the past nineteen years. Oh yes, I knew lots of things about God from an intellectual perspective. I believed with all my heart that everything in Nature was a manifestation of God, even humanity. I had studied extensively and meditated regularly, but was lacking any significant personal experience of the love of God.

I believe God's purpose for bringing Glory into my experience was to let me know She had felt my love for Her and the conscious yearning of my heart. Glory's manifestation was a tangible acknowledgment of God's unbounded love for me. Just how unusual and remarkable Glory's behavior actually was would soon be made even more apparent by the reactions of the native Fijians living in Viani Bay.

Chapter 4

A VISITOR FROM VIANI BAY

Glory was nowhere to be seen the next day, but we had a visitation of the human variety. I heard the putt, putt, putt of the one-cylinder, two-stroke diesel engine before I actually saw the *I Loi* come 'round the reef at the western tip of Vodovodonabolo Bay. *I Loi* was native Fijian Jack Fisher's twenty-foot wooden boat, painted white with green trim. Jack's father had been English and his mother was one hundred percent Fijian, making Jack and his six siblings *kailoma*, or half Fijian and half European.

Jack was gregarious, to say the least. The good news was that his English was excellent, enabling us to communicate at deep levels, rather than the superficial conversation that frequently occurs with people who speak a different language. We were excited to see Jack again and heartily welcomed him aboard *Dreamer*, once the *I Loi* was properly secured by her bow line, or painter, to our stern.

"Well, how long are you planning to stay here?" he asked as he picked up a second macaroon to accompany his cup of tea. To our surprise, he explained that he knew of our arrival the day we anchored in Vodovodonabolo Bay.

"I want you to know, Jack, that I *truly* appreciate your giving us these two weeks of heavenly solitude, but I'm curious, how did you know that we were here?"

"Surely you remember that I operate a taxi service on the *I Loi* out of Viani Bay over to Taveuni Island, so the villagers can shop for soap and tea and sugar and such. On the way back, I saw you navigating *Dreamer* into this bay."

"I'll be darned. I should have known."

"I wasn't *totally* sure it was your boat, but I was pretty sure, so I verified it on my next trip. Then I told Sofi you were here, but we decided to leave you alone for a little while. But more than two weeks! It's high time that you get over to Viani Bay. By now, everyone knows that you're here and we've all been waiting for your return."

"Jack, I've got to tell you the most incredible thing. There's this giant triggerfish here in Vodovodonabolo Bay. It swam up to the surface to greet us as soon as we dropped our hook and it's just gorgeous. Not only that, it's friendly and even swims with me. You just won't believe this until you see it for yourself."

I stood up and looked around for Glory, but she wasn't in sight. "Jack, I named this fish Glory for the glory of God in all creation, and I communicate with her telepathically. Look, here's a sketch I drew of her."

"I know this type of fish," Jack said, studying my sketch, "and they make very good eating. You remember Abu Covert, my cousin? From time to time he spears one of these giant triggerfish and they are quite delicious. Also, they're very aggressive so it's really hard for me to believe that one of them would befriend a human being like you're describing. Now, I'm not saying I don't believe you, but..."

"Well, I'm not lying to you, Jack. Glory has never acted aggressively towards me. I just hope you'll have the opportunity to see for yourself sometime. Rog, tell him about Glory, would you?"

"I will only say that Glory hangs around *Dreamer* a lot. Deb tells me she's been swimming with this fish the past two mornings, but I wasn't topsides to see this for myself. Sometimes Glory comes back in the early evening, and I see her swimming around *Dreamer*. Deb feeds her some stale bread occasionally. What I do know for sure is that Debby is totally enthralled with Glory." Rog refilled Jack's tea as the Fijian helped himself to another macaroon. "Anyway, how is everyone in Viani Bay? Why isn't Sofi with you? Is she all right? And how's your mother?"

For the next half hour we got the low-down on all of the villagers. Essentially, life in Viani Bay sounded pretty much the same as when we left eleven months ago. Jack had sold a plot of land inherited from his father to a young Australian couple. The land was located about seven miles away from Viani Bay, up the east coast of Vanua Levu. "I want to take you there to meet Phil and Tamara. Their one year-old baby, Jocko, is our godson, and we just adore him!"

"That sounds great," Rog said. "We'd love to go. I'll tell you what. If Deb can pull herself away from Glory, we'll weigh anchor tomorrow afternoon and come on over to Viani Bay by dinner time tomorrow. How's that sound?"

"It's high time, I'd say. And enough of these fish stories!" Jack sported an ear to ear grin below his sun-bleached mustache and his eyes twinkled merrily in his square, ruddy face. His brown wavy hair was cut in a Western style and at forty-four years of age, was receding on both the left and right sides of his forehead. A heart attack victim, Jack had been forced to curtail his physical activities and now weighed in at about two hundred seventy-five pounds. Nonetheless, his weight was all muscle. In one smooth motion, he untied the *I Loi's* painter from our stern, pulled it along-side *Dreamer*, and agilely jumped on board. He started his diesel engine and was underway.

As the *I Loi* rounded the tip of Vodovodonabolo Bay, I began tidying up *Dreamer* for our departure the next day. I hoped to spend some time with Glory before leaving and I was a bit concerned that she hadn't come to visit us all day.

I was on deck by 6:30 the next morning, knowing that might well be my final opportunity to interact with Glory. I was hoping she would sense our rapidly approaching departure and grace me with her presence. And sure enough, she was there in the water waiting for me. I spent some time gazing down at Glory from the stern, making sure my drawing accurately captured her beauty. I was satisfied that I had done so, especially considering my meager artistic capabilities.

I decided two things. I would try swimming with fins this time, and I would feed Glory a piece of bread before entering the water. I retrieved my flippers from the starboard lazarette locker in the cockpit, then hurried below to cut a piece of bread. When I came back up to the cockpit, she was gone. My disappointment, almost panic in fact, and my self-recrimination for leaving the scene was acute. Mentally I lashed out with urgency, "*Glory, come back, PLEASE. This could be our last day together, ever.*"

Within three minutes she was back, thank heavens. Gratefully and lovingly I fed her the bread, feasting my eyes on her every movement through the water. When the bread was gone, I put on my flippers and eased myself down the ladder while Glory watched, expectantly, so I thought. She was right there with me in total trust when I came down the ladder. Glory was beginning a ritual. I would stay fairly still in the water, looking at her and sending her my love and appreciation while she would swim very close to me, then turn and lead me off on some adventure.

With my flippers on, I could dive more quickly and easily when Glory began to descend to a bommie. However she didn't seem to like it, and disappeared. I remembered what Jack had told me the day before about Abu Covert spearing giant triggerfish, and I decided that was the reason Glory got spooked whenever I dove. I snorkeled over to her bommie, hoping to find her there. Sure enough, there she was on the top of it with a small blue cleaner fish called a wrasse clinging to the side of her mouth. She seemed proud of this, maneuvering her body so I could clearly see the little cleaner fish clinging to her.

Glory swam away to the left and took me right past a small manta ray. I sent her a message, *"Boy, that was neat, Glory! Thank you!"*

I got psyched to dive down again and try to follow her underwater, so I did a shallow dive as I swam forward after her but once again she got spooked and disappeared. So I snorkeled over to her bommie and dove down onto the top of it, hoping Glory would see how harmless I was underwater. She wasn't there, but I figured she was watching from somewhere. I dove down twice hoping she'd reappear, but she didn't, so I snorkeled back to *Dreamer*, took off my fins and climbed the boarding ladder, feeling confident that she would reappear shortly.

And as soon as I was toweled off, there she was. I fed Glory a second piece of bread, all the while telling her this was our last morning together and how much I was going to miss her. Long after the bread was gone, she continued to hang around our stern, swimming within a foot of the hull, while I continued to gawk at her and communicate telepathically. *"If I never see you again, Glory, I thank you a million times for our experiences together, and I feel sure that I will see you again in my dreams. My Spirit bows to God in Thee."* Finally she left. It was just before 8:00 a.m.

By now Rog was up and ready to eat breakfast and spring into action. Playing cards, cribbage board, dominos, books, guitar, camera and writing materials were easily stowed. I ran the dust cloth over our teak interior while Rog cleared off the chart table. After breakfast, I tidied up the galley. Up on deck, Rog lashed down our water and diesel jugs while I stowed my snorkeling gear. Then we relaxed for a while.

When we knew it was time to leave our hideaway, Rog reluctantly pulled *Gos* up alongside our starboard side. We did this to ensure that her painter would not get wrapped around the propeller, in case *Dreamer's* anchor chain got wrapped around a bommie and we had to maneuver her free. Since we ran our diesel engine every day to draw down the temperature in our refrigerator and freezer, it was ready to go at the turn of the key. As we left Vodovodonabolo Bay at 1:15 that afternoon, I bid Glory a thousand good-byes.

Chapter 5

WELCOMING PARTY

We had near-perfect weather during our entire stay in Glory's Cove, and this day was no exception. Just to be on the safe side, I stood up on the bow pulpit to watch for bommies and Rog eased out the painter for *Gos*, allowing the dinghy to drift behind *Dreamer* in towing position. I felt so blessed to be in this tropical paradise where beauty surrounded us on all sides. Northeastern Fiji was graced with periods of heavy tropical rainfall that covered the islands in lush, green vegetation. Swaying coconut palms provided the canopy for smaller lemon, papaya and banana trees and the white terns stood out clearly against the royal blue sky as they performed their aerobatic dances for us.

Ahead and five nautical miles across Somosomo Strait stood the majestic island of Taveuni, her mountainous spine reminding me of an ancient brontosaurus. Once settled in Viani Bay, we'd need to utilize Jack's water taxi service to restock some of our staples from the stores on Taveuni.

As we withdrew from Vodovodonabolo Bay around the outer coral tip, we felt the outgoing current in Somosomo Strait add two knots to our forward speed. The current runs fast there, which is why the gorgeous soft corals proliferate. I looked forward to scuba diving the Rainbow Reef as we had done the year before and Jack had promised that he'd take us on the *I Loi*.

Passing around the tip of the western reef of Glory's Cove, we turned to starboard and entered the outer reaches of Viani Bay. The village lay three nautical miles ahead. It was just as beautiful as Vodovodonabolo Bay because contrary to Western development, the small Fijian huts, called *bures,* have thatched roofs and blend quietly into the natural environment. They were not even noticeable until we reached the head of the bay, about a half hour later. Again, the beaches were almost white, a striking contrast with the spring green of the vegetation, the shimmering turquoise of the bay, and the clear blue of the sky.

Dreamer had been spotted on the way in. A welcoming committee led by Jack and Sofi Fisher and Sofi's daughter Loi headed toward us in their outboard skiff, laden with people, pawpaws, bananas and eggplant.

Jack indicated a safe place for us to drop anchor. Once that was accomplished, we welcomed them all aboard: Jack, Sofi, Loi, Ed and Aseta Fisher, Abu Covert and a beautiful tall woman with high cheekbones and flawless skin that we didn't know. In addition to the fresh produce, Sofi brought some home-brewed iced tea, together with sweet banana bread still warm from her wood-burning oven.

As soon as her arms were free, Sofi and I enjoyed a warm, excited embrace. Even though she was young enough to be my daughter, this tiny Fijian woman, twenty-eight years old, was more like a younger sister to me. We'd had so much fun together last year that I knew she, too, was anticipating a renewal of the rapport we'd shared.

Sofi and I set food and beverages on our drop-leaf table and the nine of us settled comfortably into our cockpit. The noise was deafening as everyone chattered at once. When our guests calmed down, Abu introduced us to Andrea Lumkon, his girlfriend. Andrea had moved to Viani Bay from Suva about six months earlier so that she and Abu could explore their relationship further. Ed and Aseta were the lay ministers at the village Methodist Church. Of course, they wanted to make certain we were planning to attend the Sunday morning service. We assured them we'd be there.

Loi had turned thirteen while we were in New Zealand, and although thin like her mother, she was beginning to show signs of womanhood. We were soon to learn, however, that her endearing impish behavior had not changed much.

"Loi, I thought you'd be in parochial school over on Taveuni by now," I said.

"Well, I am, but we're on spring break right now and don't go back until two days after Fiji Day."

"I've forgotten—could you please remind me when Fiji Day is?"

"October 9th."

"How about inviting some of your friends for a picnic on board *Dreamer* like we did last year? As long as your mother will agree to come along as chaperone, that is. Sofi?"

"Of course, of course. The kids have great fun last year."

"Fiji Day is still seventeen days away, so we won't worry about it now. Just tell your friends that we'll be going again and whoever can come is invited."

"Great! I'll tell them all."

Turning to Abu, I asked, "How many fish have you speared recently?"

"I got about twenty a few nights ago, and a dozen before that."

"Are you still going over to Taveuni to work with your father?"

"Not too much, especially since Andrea arrived. We moved into the Homestead here and I hang out with Uncle Jack, helping him with the grounds, shopping trips and fishing, while Andrea helps Sofi with the house chores."

I glanced at the tall, attractive woman beside him. Her features distinguished her from every other Fijian woman I had met, in particular her height and the honey blonde color of her hair, pulled back tightly and circled on top of her head in a bun. She intrigued me, and I hoped to learn more about her during our visit. I couldn't help but wonder why Abu and Andrea were a twosome. He was a nice looking young man, of medium stature, while she was so tall and dramatic. My curiosity was piqued.

Casting a loving gaze over at Sofi who was trying to keep Loi from eating the last of the banana bread, I called to her, "Come on over here, you little rascal!" Loi thought I was talking to her and bounded over in typical Loi style. Landing on my lap, the top of her head, covered with short, curly black hair, was only a half-inch below the top of my own head.

"You are really growing up, young lady!" I exclaimed.

"Yes, and she play volleyball very good," said Sofi proudly.

"How are your grades, Loi?" I asked. "You know how hard your Mom and Dad work to pay for your schooling."

"Yes, I know, but I don't know what my grades are yet. They didn't hand them out to us before spring break."

"The teacher say she doing okay when we pick her up on Friday," Sofi said.

"Loi, you're getting too big to sit on my lap now. How 'bout getting up and pouring me another glass of your mother's delicious iced tea."

With that I sat back and relaxed while everyone continued sharing for another half hour. As evening approached, everyone knew it was time to go and one-by-one, they stepped down into the *I Loi*.

"Sofi, if I bring in about four bags of laundry tomorrow, can you help me wash it all?" I asked.

"Of course. Come early, because it take long time to do much clothes."

"And I'll help Rog burn the trash," added Jack just before he started the little diesel engine and pushed the *I Loi* off from *Dreamer*.

"*Vinaka vaka levu.*"

"You're welcome."

"*Moce mada.*"

"Good-bye and see you all later, too."

Chapter 6

THE HOMECOMING

"Wake up, Rog. No sleeping in this morning. I can see Jack and Sofi on the beach waiting for us."

After our guests left *Dreamer* the previous evening, I got all of our dirty clothes together and Rog piled the plastic bags of non-biodegradable trash into the cockpit. We needed only to eat a quick breakfast, put on some clothes and throw the bags of dirty clothes and trash into *Gos* before going ashore. For Rog, getting dressed amounted to donning shorts and a T-shirt, but women in Fiji have to wear sarongs, skirts or dresses in the villages or cities. The native women in Viani Bay typically wore sarongs with T-shirts.

"Okay, okay, give me another five minutes. I'm still half asleep." I kissed him on the cheek. After putting on my purple and white sundress, I scurried to the galley and cut open one of the perfectly ripened pawpaws gifted to us yesterday. I cracked open the last of our Vaseline-protected eggs and before scrambling them, reawakened Rog. "Eggs are about to go into the pan," I chided.

"Okay, I'm vertical."

"Good. Try to keep moving."

I realized how much I enjoyed the galley, with its three propane burners; stainless steel, under-the-counter refrigerator and freezer; deep double sinks and lots of counter space—a luxury not claimed by many with yachts our size. As it was open to the main salon, *Dreamer's* galley was my first introduction to cooking in a great room. Our large drop-leaf table, along with the forward bulkhead beyond the navy blue settee and the chart table, filled this space with the soft, honey-brown warmth of pampered and well-oiled teak. *Dreamer* was so cozy it truly felt like home to us.

Just as the eggs were ready, Rog appeared. "I'm so glad you love to cook now."

"Yep, it's a whole different experience for me here on the boat," I replied happily. "But we'd best not linger. Do you hear Jack whistling to us?"

Five minutes later we were in *Gos*, surrounded by bags of trash and laundry, heading for the white crescent beach of Viani Bay. Jack and Sofi waved enthusiastically, then waded out to help us unload the dinghy and haul her ashore. That accomplished, I threw my arms around Sofi's waist and lifted her into the air. She squealed delightedly and I said, "This is the proper hug I didn't have a chance to give to you yesterday." Sofi stands all of about four feet, eleven inches high and can honestly be called skinny. I planned to ask her someday why she had so little meat on her bones compared with the other Fijian woman. Next to Jack, she practically looked like a midget. I just loved the two of them to death and was so happy to be back in Viani Bay to share many happy days with them.

"*Lako i sili*," Sofi said with a big laugh.

"*Lako i sili* yourself," I responded. I had forgotten all about this Fijian phrase that Sofi now teased me with. The literal translation is go and take your bath, which might have originated from the fact that Fijian huts don't have running water.

The four of us carried the bags of trash over near the old drying rack the Fishers used to use to dry white coconut meat. This dried meat, known as copra, was then carted away by ship to be used in the production of coconut cream, desiccated coconut, coconut oil, jam, lard, candy, soap, and even meal for chicken feed. The remaining husks, coco sheaths and shells lay on the ground, waiting to be burned. They would make helpful kindling to burn our trash.

At one time, the coconut industry was a lucrative business for the Fijians. It helped them raise the money necessary to send their teenagers to the private schools originally founded by Christian missionaries. The school closest to Viani Bay was on Taveuni Island, eight miles across the bay and Somosomo Strait. But the coconut industry had seriously declined, making it difficult for the rural Fijians to raise the money these schools demanded.

Before Jack and Rog began digging the hole to burn the trash, Jack said he had something to show us. We followed him a hundred yards up a small rise to a fenced-in area containing seven piglets and a sow. Jack was clearly proud of his pigs, explaining to us that they were a new way for him to raise money and that he had already sold one to his cousins.

"Loi, what are you doing?" I asked as I watched Loi on the other side of the pigpen, pulling straight back on the tail of a five-day-old calf. She just laughed, but dropped the tail as the mama cow approached her baby.

We then walked over to the manicured lawn that sloped downwards in an emerald carpet from the main house all the way to the beach below. Sofi and Jack had left four large washtubs near the expanse of clotheslines. We each picked one up and followed Jack to the well. Sofi and I hauled up the water with the bucket connected to the well by a long line. We were in the middle of filling the washtubs with water when Jack's cousin, Marian arrived in her black dress, dotted with tiny pink blossoms. I remembered this pretty woman from the year before. Of medium height and build, her round face was softly framed by her dark brown, curly hair.

"Jack told me you were doing lots of laundry today. Can I help you?"

I was glad for her company and welcomed her with a hug. After filling all four washtubs, we helped each other carry them near the clotheslines, then poured soap into the first tub and added a bunch of clothes. I had brought my toilet plunger, my favorite tool for doing laundry. It made agitating the clothes a simple matter. The next step was to squeeze the soapy water out of the clothes, transferring them to washtub number two where they were re-agitated. This got maybe half of the soap out, especially since this was the first load and the water was fresh. We repeated this action in washtubs three and four, and by that time most of the soap was out of the clothing and the individual pieces were ready to hang on the line. It was necessary to change the water a couple of times, taking us the better part of three hours to finish the job.

Sofi delighted in breaking the monotony of washing clothes by periodically chasing me around the lawn. Twenty-one years my junior, she always caught me, whereupon we would both pretend to fall down and then tickle each other. Such fun and games made me feel like I was about thirteen years old myself, which reminded me of Loi. I wondered where Loi had disappeared to. Sofi suggested she'd probably skipped off to JJ and Jumina's home as soon as we began doing the laundry.

"Typical teenager," I said.

Around noon, we continued on up the hill to the main house, referred to as the Fisher Homestead. It was a huge house by Fijian standards, and decidedly European compared to the typical *bures* that were home to the other residents of Viani Bay. The rectangular wooden structure was painted a deep Indian red, containing ten large windows on the eastern and southern sides with solid wooden shutters that could be closed during a cyclone. The roof was metal and there was a small porch in the center of the southern side where Jack and Rog stood, watching us walk up the hill.

Jack was wearing his typical huge grin and I yelled, "Jack, I feel like I'm home." The beautifully landscaped lawn rolling down to the white sandy beach was accented with colorful Ti shrubs, other bushes and ferns. Beyond the white sandy beach was the multi-hued Viani Bay itself, its bluish-white foam where the water kissed the beach followed by a vivid turquoise, then becoming a darker royal blue as the land receded and the water grew deeper. The bay was ringed like a horseshoe with fingers of land reaching out towards Somosomo Strait on the east and on the west. Tucked into the east side of the bay was Yanuyanu Island where Ed and Aseta Fisher lived, and across Somosomo Strait was the beautiful Taveuni Island.

"Welcome home," Jack said. "It took you a long time to get here, but you're here now, so come on up and have some of Andrea's iced tea and scones."

As I mounted the steps to the porch and entered the stark living room, there sat May Fisher, the matriarch of Viani Bay. She wore a blue and white dress that complimented her curly gray, shoulder-length hair. May was a big woman, still strong at nearly eighty-one-years of age. Her broken front teeth called attention to her mouth; because of this, she tried hard not to smile too broadly.

Her large eyeglasses complimented her square face. May was mother to six sons and two daughters, all of whom remained on either Vanua Levu or Taveuni Islands. Her husband's brother, Ned, married and had five offspring, most of whom also still lived in this part of Fiji. Ed Fisher of Yanuyanu Island was one of Ned's two sons. I walked over to give May a hug and she said very simply and warmly, "Welcome, welcome."

Andrea came into the living room with iced tea, colored glasses, scones, butter, jam, knives, small plates and napkins, all on a single tray that she set down on a small table. Jack and Sofi, Rog and I, Marian, May and Andrea all helped ourselves to this favorite Fijian repast. There was a bit of silence as we devoured a couple of scones each, then the talking began. We asked May how each of her sons and daughters were doing. I couldn't catch her every word, but she seemed disgruntled about something so I made a mental note to ask Jack about that later.

After a half hour of chatting, Sofi broke out a deck of cards and Marian excused herself. Four of us began playing sweep, with the other two looking on. This game is very similar to canasta, but playing it with Jack and Sofi was absolutely hilarious. While all of us were experienced, Jack got very lucky. Sofi got so upset with his winning streak that she leaped out of her chair and began beating on Jack, who simply laughed. Rog and I cracked up watching the two of them interact. Andrea and May took their turns around the table and after a couple of hours of cards, we decided the laundry was probably dry. Sofi and I got it down fairly quickly, folding each piece and placing it back into the large plastic garbage bags it came ashore in.

I suggested that Jack and Sofi come over for dinner after we restocked at the stores in Taveuni. Jack said we were in luck because Tuesday happened to be his regular store run, and that was tomorrow.

"What time are you leaving?" Rog asked.

"We'll pick you up at 8:00 a.m.," Jack said, "so please be ready!"

"Whatever happened to Fiji time?" Rog asked.

"Everybody will be in the boat and ready to leave, so if you're not ready, we'll have to leave without you," Jack teased with that big grin on his tan face.

"Okay, okay, I'll be ready." With that promise, we walked down to *Gos* with the laundry. Jack helped to launch our dinghy, since the tide was low, and we returned to *Dreamer*.

Once on board, we shared a meager meal of rice, beans, tomato sauce and boiled Fijian spinach--nothing like American spinach—which was donated by Aseta upon our arrival. Sitting in our cockpit with the sun sinking behind us, we reviewed our first couple of days in Viani Bay. While I missed Glory and the relaxation and intimacy Rog and I shared in Vodovodonabolo Bay, we realized how fortunate we were to have this opportunity to share our lives with such generous and loving people in one of the most beautiful settings in the world. It almost seemed too perfect. We were soon to learn that people are people, complete with emotions and conflicts, no matter where on the globe they live.

That night, however, we were oblivious to any turmoil. We felt only the loving presence of God within all creation. In that contentment, we cuddled in our double bunk, our passion capping off what Rog referred to as "yet another shitty day in paradise."

Chapter 7

SEVENTEEN IN A SMALL BOAT

At 8:00 sharp the following morning, the *I Loi* approached *Dreamer* with fifteen people on board. Abu held *Dreamer* as Rog handed down two empty five-gallon gasoline jugs for our dinghy's outboard motor and four empty six-gallon water jugs. It was a beautiful calm morning and after shoving off from *Dreamer*, the *I Loi* seemed to smile happily as she chugged along with all of her passengers. I climbed up onto the rooftop with Sofi, and Andrea politely went below to be with Abu, giving Sofi and me a chance to chat.

I looked at my very dear little friend, so full of life and energy that she virtually sparkled with enthusiasm, at least whenever we were together. She had thick, long black curly hair that she usually pulled back softly, so there was still fullness around her face. Her eyes were brown and always sparkled, like Jack's. Halfway up her thin left forearm, she wore a gold watch that Jack had given to her, and on her left hand, between the base of her thumb and her index finger, was a faded black tattoo. "Let me see that tattoo, Sofi. What does it say?" She extended her left hand to me, but I must have been looking at the tattoo the wrong way, because I couldn't make it out.

"It say JF," Sofi responded.

"What's that stand for?" I asked naively.

"Jack Fisher," she said blushing through her naturally browned complexion.

"Of course!" I said. "What a dodo I am."

"Yes, you is a dodo," she said laughing. She seemed to like that expression.

"Sofi, will you tell me why you are so much shorter and thinner than all of the other Fijian women I've met."

"My mother die when I am only two months old. She sick all the time she pregnant with me, so I am born runt. I am raised by my Auntie in Raviravi Village."

"Where is Raviravi Village?"

"On north shore of Vanua Levu Island."

I knew that was pretty far away, especially without a car, because Viana Bay was on the southern shore of the large Vanua Levu Island.

"How did you meet Jack, then?" I asked.

"He come to Raviravi Village looking for partner, and he ask me if I will come to Viani Bay with him."

"Really! Were you glad he asked you? Were you afraid of leaving all of the people you grew up with?"

"Yes, I am afraid, but I am excited, too."

"How old were you when this happened?"

"I twenty and Loi five."

"What about Loi's father?"

"We not married and we not living together so no problem. My Auntie think it good thing for Loi if we come to Viani Bay with Jack to be a family."

"Are you happy, now, that you made that decision?"

"Yes…." It was a very hesitant yes, so I asked Sofi another question.

"So, did you and Jack get married soon after you came to Viani Bay?"

"No, we not married."

"Why not?"

"He still married to first wife."

"No! Why?"

"He say he ask her for divorce many times, but she say no."

"Why not? Do I know her? Where is she living?"

"She live in Suva with their two daughters who grown up now. When Jack first meet you in restaurant last year in Suva, he is visiting his daughters."

"Did he see his wife then, too?"

"Yes, he tell me he ask her again for divorce."

"And why won't she give him one?"

"Because she know Jack supposed to inherit the Fisher Homestead and she want more money."

"What about Jack's other brothers and his sisters? Won't they get some of the land, too?"

"Jack supposed to get Homestead because he live here and take care of mother and land. Brothers and sisters take care of own families and houses. Too busy for mother."

"Oh, Sofi, I'm so sorry."

"Well, Jack very good to Loi and me. I work very hard with cooking and washing and cleaning, but Jack love us both, and he adopt Loi as his own daughter. Jack and I have bedroom at house, too."

"You know, I just got a thought. Maybe after the New Year, we can all go to Savusavu together on *Dreamer*. Can you get to Raviravi Village from there?"

"Yes! And you come to my home village with me and Loi and meet my Auntie!"

"Oh, Sofi, that would be so much fun. Let me talk with Rog about it and see if he'll agree."

We lay on our bellies on the nice warm rooftop with our heads close together, cushioned on our hands. The gentle rocking of the boat and the drone of the diesel engine lured us to sleep for maybe half an hour. Soon we approached Taveuni, awakened by the noise of Abu getting ready to set the anchor. The wooden skiff we towed across Somosomo Strait was too small for seventeen people, so we went ashore in three shifts. In Fijian, Jack told the other passengers when to be back for our return trip.

While Rog, Jack and Abu went off with the jerry jugs, Sofi, Andrea and I went to the small produce store. I brought our canvas bags with me and loaded them with carrots, lettuce, tomatoes, garlic, onions, potatoes, green beans, green peppers, red peppers, pumpkin squash, cabbage, butter and eggs. I did not buy any of the fruit, eggplants or Fijian spinach that are grown in Viani Bay.

We went on to the store that sold packaged food next, and I stocked up on Spam, peanut butter and jelly, bread, mayonnaise, mustard, curry powder, brown rice, beans, tuna fish, spaghetti and sauce, three jars of Planters peanuts and soap. Finally, we went to the fish and meat store. Sofi told me not to buy any fish because Abu would bring us whatever we needed, so I only bought ten pounds of chicken pieces and six steaks that I could vacuum seal with our Food Saver and freeze back on our boat. We took all of our provisions to Lesuma Holdings, an enterprise owned by friends of Jack and Sofi's, who kindly refrigerated the steaks, chicken and fresh produce for me.

Next, we walked to a variety store where Sofi and Andrea bought some fabric and thread. I noticed that they had coloring books, crayons, cards and blank audio cassette tapes, storing that information away because I was already thinking ahead to Christmas presents.

Sofi and Andrea led me off to The Cannibal Café where we were scheduled to meet Jack, Abu and Rog for lunch. This delightful restaurant had a covered patio on the waterfront with a sign that read, "The Cannibal Café:

We Love to Have You For Dinner!" Eating there became a tradition for us whenever we made shopping trips to Taveuni.

Jack charged five Fijian dollars for the round-trip fare, and he made the run twice a week. This was another way he made a little money to send Loi to school.

We were back at the loading site by 3:00 and everyone else was waiting there for us. Soon all seventeen of us, plus all of the packages and the now heavy jerry jugs were aboard. It was a rough ride in the unprotected waters of Somosomo Strait and we were all glad when we finally entered the outer limits of Viani Bay into smoother water. When we came alongside *Dreamer*, Jack lifted those heavy jerry jugs up to us as if they were mere toys. In other ports of call, it was always a struggle for us to handle them ourselves.

"*Vinaka vaka levu*," we called out to Jack in thanks.

"*Sega na leqa*," or no worries, he replied.

"*Moce*," we said to everyone as we waved good-bye.

Chapter 8

CONCERNS REVEALED

The next day as we were enjoying a late breakfast in the cockpit, Jack came across the water rowing his wooden skiff.

"*Ni sa yandra*, Jack," which means good morning. "Come on aboard." I ladled two large spoonfuls of sourdough banana pancake batter onto the griddle while Rog tied the *I Loi* painter to our port aft cleat.

"Where's Sofi?" I asked.

"She's working around the house today."

"That's what I've got to do myself. I have to vacuum seal and stow all of that food we bought yesterday. Do you and Sofi want to come on board for dinner tonight?"

"That would be great," Jack said as I handed up two pancakes to him.

"Tell us about Abu and Andrea. They're so quiet around us that I don't feel like I know them at all."

"Well, Abu met her in Suva, and he was smitten immediately. I don't know whether it's going to work out or not. She's quite a handful for him, but for now she seems content. She says she has some Swedish blood in her and when she lived in Suva, she tried modeling, but it didn't work out. Andrea has some high-falutin' ideas, but Abu tends to keep her grounded. Do you know that he takes her out snorkeling at night when he goes spearfishing?"

"No. I replied. "Isn't that pretty brave for a Fijian woman? I know that all Fijian women are hard-working and they do a lot of net fishing, but I haven't noticed any of the women actually swimming."

"You're right," Jack said. "That's a rare thing."

"I'd like to take Sofi someday. I think she'd enjoy it."

"She'll enjoy it all right if she doesn't drown!"

"Well, I'll start her out in shallow water or near a reef that I can stand on."

"There's a reef just north of Yanuyanu Island that you might try. Then if you're drowning, you can yell out for Eddie, Jr. and he'll come rescue the two of you."

"Thanks for your confidence in me, Jack!"

I had decided to keep the meal simple, spaghetti and a salad, but lots of both because I'd seen Jack eat and he can definitely stow it away. Dinner was ready by the time Jack came back to *Dreamer* with Sofi. I served the meal inside around our large table so that Sofi could be comfortable on our settee. After the meal, which lasted only about fifteen minutes, Jack said, "Sofi, get up and help Debby."

"No, Jack," I replied. "Sofi is our guest and she is to rest and enjoy herself."

"Okay, if you say so."

"Yes, I say so. Now here are the movies we think you would enjoy the most." Rog handed him a pile of VHS tapes. Happily, Sofi stretched out on the port-side settee with my dolphin-decorated pillow under her head while Jack, like a kid in a candy store, eagerly looked through the tapes. He chose "Hunt for Red October" and "Crocodile Dundee," two of our personal favorites. Although we had already seen each of them twice, I enjoyed watching them again if for no other reason than to share Jack's vibrant enthusiasm. Sofi fell fast asleep after the first ten minutes and Rog hit the bunk after the first movie.

At the end of "Crocodile Dundee," Jack felt like talking, so I attentively listened to some of his concerns. When he began talking about the Fisher Homestead, I was careful not to reveal what Sofi had already told me, intuiting that she might be reprimanded for disclosing insider information to me. I was surprised when Jack told me that although he had an arrangement with his mother to inherit the Fisher Homestead after her death, he feared that his older brothers were plotting against his inheritance.

"What makes you say that, Jack?"

"They aren't happy that I sold my inherited land to Phil and Tamara. My brothers are afraid I'll sell the Homestead after Mom dies."

"Would you do that?"

"Of course not! It is our family land and the best piece of property still in my father's name."

"Did you tell your brothers this?"

"Yes I did, but I heard a rumor in Taveuni yesterday that my three oldest brothers, Sesel, Bertie and Chris, hired an attorney last week."

"Maybe you should talk with your mother?"

"I think she is beginning to feel the way they feel."

"Can you promise to her that you won't sell the Homestead, no matter what?"

"I've told her that before, but maybe I'll say something to her again."

"Maybe you could talk with your brothers again, too. Why did you sell your land?"

"To help support Mom and take care of the Homestead. You know there's no business or industry here in Viani Bay, so it's difficult for us to acquire any money to repair the house, to send Loi to school or for doctors if we ever need them, especially for Mom as she ages. We need money to buy some supplies on Taveuni and if we ever want to go anywhere, that costs money, too, even for fuel for the *I Loi*."

"Jack, try to think positively and be sure to say some prayers for peace, harmony and right understanding."

"Okay. Thanks for listening."

He gave me a big bear hug. Then I went out into the cockpit, untied the wooden skiff from *Dreamer* and pulled her alongside while Jack woke up Sofi and led her half asleep up to the cockpit, where he helped her down into the skiff. Quietly we said good-bye. I blessed them silently as they pulled away and Jack rowed towards the beach. I hoped Rog and I could bring light and love into their lives and somehow be a positive influence on the family at large.

It was a delicate balance between being a good listener and occasionally offering advice. We weren't that familiar with all of the nuances of their culture and we certainly didn't believe in interfering with the lives of our hosts. On the other hand, we did believe in praying for all of them and for God's will, not ours, to be done.

Both Rog and I believe that God always knows what is best for everyone in the long run. Sometimes we don't like the lessons that we have to learn, and what we have to go through to learn them. But in every aspect of our own lives, we've seen in retrospect that God, in His infinite wisdom, knew what He was doing all along.

Chapter 9

UNDERWATER GARDEN OF EDEN

In the mid 1990's, Viani Bay was off the beaten track, mostly unknown by the yachting community at large. We learned about it from our good friends on *Sundowner*. After visiting there in 1994, we enlightened some other yachting friends, the owners of *Romper* and *Legacy* who'd shared a dock with us in Nelson, New Zealand from November 1994 through May 1995.

Early one sunny afternoon, we were onboard with Jack and Sofi when we heard the crackle of our VHF radio. *"Dreamer, Dreamer,* this is the sailing vessel *Romper.* Do you copy?"

"Romper, Romper, this is *Dreamer.* Where are you, Rik?"

I listened to his crisp reply. "According to the chart, we're only a nautical mile east of the entrance to Viani Bay and Ann is up in the bosun's chair, keeping an eye out for coral heads."

"Welcome to Viani Bay," I replied. "Keep Ann up the mast because there are also a couple of bommies near the head of the Bay where we're anchored. After you drop the hook and get settled, give us another shout and we'll ferry you over to *Dreamer*. There are some people on board we'd like you to meet."

"Sounds great. *Romper* out."

"*Dreamer* standing by."

"Who's that?" Sofi asked.

"Our good friends, Rik and Ann Allen. I think you'll really like them. Ann has a smile as wide as a mile and Rik is a real down-to-earth kind of guy who can fix just about anything. They are Canadians from Ontario who spent many years in the Caribbean before taking *Romper* through the Panama Canal and crossing the Big Pond to reach the South Pacific. Ann is a master diver and she and Rik taught scuba diving during their years in the Caribbean."

"Really?" Jack asked. Before his heart attack, Jack free dove regularly among the bommies in Somosomo Strait, fishing to feed his extended family.

"Yes," I answered, "and Rog and I have been itching to go diving again ourselves. Can we hire you and the *I Loi* to take us out for some drift dives?"

76

"I'm ready to go!" Jack replied. "When are we leaving?"

"Well, tomorrow is Sunday and Ed and Aseta are expecting us in church." I had a plan in mind about the scuba diving but didn't voice it.

"So it is, and it's also my mother's eighty-first birthday. How 'bout you and your friends joining us for Sunday dinner at the Homestead after church?"

Just then, *Romper* was pulling back on her anchor, fifty yards off our starboard stern, to insure a secure set. Cupping my hands over my mouth, I called out from our stern, letting my words drift back on the gentle air currents. "Are you ready for a lift?"

"We will be by the time you get here," Rik yelled back. Sofi and I hopped into our dinghy. I started the eight horsepower Evinrude outboard engine and in no time we were alongside *Romper*.

"*Bula, bula,*" Sofi and I said in unison, offering the traditional Fijian welcome as Ann jumped into *Gos* clad in a tank top and beige shorts. The Fijian rule about women wearing dresses, skirts or sarongs applied to yachties only when going ashore. Ann's coral tank top accentuated the blush of her suntanned face and her beautiful pearly white teeth. Rik was as lean as ever, dressed in one of his many short-sleeved plaid shirts and a pair of comfortable-looking khaki shorts.

"Rik and Ann, this is my very dear friend, Sofi Fisher. Sofi, meet Rik and Ann." Sofi was more reserved than I'd seen her since our arrival in Viani Bay. After reboarding *Dreamer*, she sat quietly, listening to everyone else chatter after we introduced the Allens to Jack.

We learned that *Romper* had buddy-boated up the Tasman Sea and over to Tonga with the sailing vessel *Legacy*, owned by Paul and Dianne Holmes. They had experienced an exhilarating passage after which the two couples explored all three of the Tongan Island groups of Tongatapu, the Ha'apai Group and Vava'u. We asked about our Tongan friends, Vika and Selina in Vava'u. Rik surprised us with the news that they had attended Selina's wedding to Graeme Woodroffe, a yachtsman from New Zealand who stole Selina's heart the year before while we were visiting. We listened delightedly to all the details of the wedding.

Subsequently, *Romper* and *Legacy* sailed westward to Suva, exploring the southern islands of Ono and Kandavu where they enjoyed free diving with the natives. Not owning an air compressor, they were unable to scuba dive without paying tourist prices, which they could ill afford. I eagerly suggested my plan. "Tomorrow is Sunday, and we'd love to have you join us at church. Afterward, we're all invited to Jack and Sofi's for a special Sunday dinner in celebration of Jack's mother's birthday."

"Thanks so much, Jack and Sofi." Ann smiled warmly at them.

"Jack, can we take our scuba diving trip to the Rainbow Reef Monday morning?" I asked. Ann and Rik's eyes lit up when Jack responded with an enthusiastic, "Sure!"

Decisions made, we dispersed. Jack and Sofi needed to make preparations for Mom's birthday party. Rog took Rik and Ann back to *Romper* and the men returned to *Dreamer* with the Allens' two dive tanks. Rog and Rik busied themselves hauling and setting up *Dreamer's* compressor on deck and filling the four tanks. This rather noisy, drawn-out procedure took the remainder of the afternoon. Ann and I prepared baked goods and pasta salads for a picnic lunch on board the *I Loi* after scuba diving. Jack loved to eat, so in addition to money for his services and the *I Loi's* fuel, we always celebrated our time with him via plenty of good food.

While we dined on board *Dreamer*, Rik and Ann filled us in on *Legacy*. "We radioed *Legacy* before coming over for dinner and told Dianne and Paul that we're here with you," Ann said. "They're excited to see you and hope to arrive in a couple of days."

"I'm really looking forward to seeing them again. How did they do on their twelve-hundred-mile maiden passage to Tonga from Nelson?"

"Well, Paul got seasick and Dianne had to skipper *Legacy* seventy-five percent of the time. She did fantastically well; Paul is so proud of her. They are hooked on cruising now and hope to do the May to November trip to the islands as often as possible. Which reminds me, it's already October. We want to sail west to snorkel the Blue Lagoon in northwestern Fiji before heading back to New Zealand," Rik said. "Are you sailing back to Nelson for cyclone season?"

Rog explained our plan to stay in Fiji until May, then sail on to Vanuatu, the Solomon Islands and the Louisiade Archipelago of Papau New Guinea before continuing on to Australia in November of '96. After some more small talk, we called it a night.

The following morning at 8:30, we picked up Rik and Ann and took them ashore, carrying *Gos* up above the high tide line and tying her painter to a tree before heading on up to the Fisher Homestead. We were decked out in our Sunday finery, consisting of a simple skirt and blue blouse for Ann; a printed wraparound skirt with a gold-colored blouse for me; a straw hat, plaid shirt and tan shorts for Rik; and a white and blue Hawaiian shirt tucked neatly into a solid navy blue *sulu* for Rog. A *sulu* is formal attire for Fijian males, basically a wraparound skirt in a rich, woven fabric. Rog had purchased his *sulu* from a fine men's clothing store in Suva.

We all walked up the gentle hill to the Fisher Homestead and Sofi escorted us down the well-worn path, lined with gorgeous green, yellow, orange and red Ti shrubs, to the white clapboard church seventy-five yards from the water's edge. The Fijians were attired in their finest clothing but Roger really stood out, a Caucasian male in a Fijian *sulu*. Several men approached Rog, complimenting him on his choice of *sulu*, so we felt that the villagers were impressed and pleased.

Upon entering the one-room church, we were ushered to the second bench on the left-hand side of the sanctuary. All the youngsters sat on the floor in front of the first pew with their parents in that pew where they could keep an eye on their offspring. Ed and Aseta Fisher opened the service in very good English, welcoming Rik and Ann as well as Rog and me. Explaining that a visiting pastor would be leading the actual worship service, they apologized that the remainder of the service would be conducted in the Fijian language.

As was typical of many of the tropical island services we'd attended, we did not understand the words but we easily caught the spirit of the people, their devotion and reverence. We were impressed with the superb behavior of the children as they sat quietly, modeling obedience, patience and respect.

After the service, one family after the other approached us, many of whom remembered Rog and me from the year before. We relearned their names and introduced the Allens to each family. Finally we headed back to the Homestead. Sofi led us first to the *lovo* Jack had dug the night before. Various meats and vegetables wrapped securely in palm fronds had been placed in the pit early that morning, to bake slowly. Jack extracted the fragrant, steaming hot chicken and pork, then the vegetables. Filling several large woven baskets, we made our way up the hill to the house.

The Homestead dining room was decorated with huge palm fronds placed here and there around the room. May was dressed in a pink frock. I went straight to her; wishing her a very happy eighty-first birthday and leaving Rog to pull up the rear. She smiled widely, despite her broken teeth, saying, "Welcome to you and your friends. I'm glad you could all come." I introduced both Rik and Ann around the room to the relatives I knew, including Jack's oldest brother and his wife.

Jack passed around a bowl of tiny red peppers, encouraging each of us to enjoy one. As soon as the pepper hit my mouth, I pulled it away, but not before my lower lip went totally numb. Rog's eyes began watering profusely as he cried out, "Holy mackerel! My whole mouth is on fire!" The Fijians laughed heartily at these wimpy Americans, but many of them also commented favorably about Roger's *sulu*.

From the corner of my eye, I noticed Andrea and Sofi approaching. In her hands, Andrea held the most beautiful lei I'd ever seen—mostly white frangipani blossoms, complemented by red hibiscus and bright green leaves. Andrea handed it carefully to Sofi, who garlanded an astonished Roger, kissing him on both cheeks and wishing him a happy fifty-seventh birthday. She explained that Andrea had made the lei especially for Rog after hearing that his birthday was October 6th, right near May's birthday. Andrea and Sofi disappeared back into the kitchen and we began smelling the mouth-watering aromas of curry and coconut. Soon, they reappeared, followed by May's personal maid, Raua, all bearing heaping platters of Fijian specialties.

Before long, the large buffet table was covered with colorful dishes and we *vavalangis*, or Anglos, were invited to start the procession around the table. Jack graciously waved a thatched fan over the food to keep any flying insects from alighting on the delicacies. Silence soon pervaded the room as we feasted.

The orange yams tasted like candy, fresh and sweet. The small eggplants held intriguing, impossible to describe taste sensations from their hours in the lovo and the chilies in the green beans started my taste buds a-quivering. The pork, smothered in coconut cream sauce, was tender and flavorful. But most delectable for me was the curried chicken with ginger, onions, eggplant and a hint of lemon.

After the meal Jack hosted the celebration for his mom, garlanding her with a lei—not a real one like Roger's—but a plastic one in pastel colors that complemented her dress. Next was a frosted cake with candles forming the shape of 81. Jack held it low for his mom to make a wish and blow out the candles, just like we do in the U.S.

Afterward, I invited Andrea to come over to *Dreamer* some night and show me how to make that delectable chicken curry dish. Then we discussed our plans for scuba diving the next day before withdrawing to the living room for several rounds of sweep. There was lots of jesting as we all took turns rotating in and out of the game, with May the only one who played throughout the entire session.

I could be mistaken, but I believe May had a terrific eighty-first birthday celebration. And Roger's lei adorned *Dreamer's* main salon for fifteen days thereafter, permeating our floating home with the unforgettable, sweet tropical fragrance of frangipani.

At 9:00 the following morning, the *I Loi* came alongside *Dreamer*. We quickly picked up Ann and Rik and headed south for the Rainbow Reef in Somosomo Strait. The tide was just turning and Jack described in knowledgeable detail what we would find below the surface. He explained that if we'd all stay together, he could follow our air bubbles from above. In this way we could do a drift dive, saving us from the expenditure of valuable air we'd otherwise have to use while swimming back upstream against a rapidly increasing current.

Our first dive was at a site the local diving community called the Fish Factory. There were reef fish everywhere, swimming in and out of the gorgeous soft corals that swayed in the current like flowers in the breeze. I was blown away by the profusion of colors: the magenta, gold and pink of the soft corals; the turquoise, pink, teal and purple of the huge parrot fish; the large blue dots covering the orange-red body of the coral grouper and the electric blue eyes of the giant clams. The regal angelfish showed off their brilliant shades of blue and gold while the red squirrel fish with their large eyes hid under ledges of coral at the deepest point of our dive, nearly eighty-five feet below the water's surface.

The highlight for me was the wall of moorish idol fish, perhaps fifty in number, swimming in synch not more than fifteen feet in front of me. Their geometric patterns of yellow, white and black vertical bands were surpassed in dramatic beauty only by the long, gracefully flowing dorsal fins streaming out behind them.

Ann demonstrated her joy by taking her regulator out of her mouth and flashing me a huge grin, her teeth still dazzling white even at sixty feet. Rik attempted the same stunt and was almost as successful as Ann, although he couldn't hold his breath very long. I felt a bit sad when Rog tapped me on the shoulder after about a half hour, signaling it was time to begin our ascent.

Once on the surface, we scrambled back aboard the *I Loi*. Almost giddy with excitement over the beauty we'd seen, we all started talking at once and Jack graciously gave us the time we needed to pour out our enthusiasm. I could feel his joy for us and also his pride in his country.

We chose The Corner and The Mini White Wall area for our second dive. We began our descent right near the International Date Line dividing the eastern and western hemispheres. The flood current was strong, making it difficult for us to get over the top of the reef to the wall. But after that the dive was terrific, yielding an array of fish from large schools to a single napoleon fish, a petrale, and a sea turtle swimming so gracefully it was hard to imagine this could be the same creature that has such a difficult time plodding up the beach to lay her eggs.

In addition to the joy of swimming with the sea turtle, what I liked most were the soft corals, ranging from a proliferation of blues and purples in the Corner area to the ledge of the Mini-White Wall, where the color changed to a vibrant white. We stayed underwater for thirty-five minutes before ascending.

After boarding the *I Loi*, Ann couldn't stop gushing over the intense beauty of the Rainbow Reef, describing the marine world she knew so very well in vivid terms that delighted us all. Jack found a good spot to set the anchor while Ann and I uncovered our picnic lunch of macaroni salad, coleslaw, a sandwich for each of the guys and the sweets we'd baked, including macaroons and brownies.

Ann and I sat on the stern of the *I Loi* feeling like soul sisters. It was just a perfect day: blue skies, a warm gentle breeze, good food, fond memories shared all around and the joy of each other's company. My only regret was that Sofi had stayed at home to work, but I was already planning other adventures that would include my dear Fijian friend.

Chapter 10

MORE ADVENTURES

Each day in Viani Bay offered a new adventure. Boarding the *I Loi*, we traveled up the east coast of Vanua Levu to meet Phil and Tamara and their one-year-old son, Jocko, who was the godson of Jack and Sofi. Their love for the infant knew no bounds, and we were also enchanted with the tow-headed boy who crawled around in his birthday suit with the dog and cats. One behavior I found curious by Western standards was Jack's delight in stretching out the penis of the infant. He explained that if Jocko grows a bigger penis, then his stature as a man among his peers is increased.

Phil and Tamara hailed from Byron Bay, Australia, a small hippy community of earthy individuals who loved to surf. Life in Byron Bay was a good preparation for their life on the relatively isolated east coast of Vanua Levu, where they needed similar skills to be self-sufficient. With the help of Jack and Sofi, they had built their own *bure* in the round with the tallest, steepest thatched roof I had ever seen. There were no interior walls, giving the home an open spacious feeling, even though by Western standards it was quite small. Native *tapa cloth*, made by pounding the bark of the mulberry bush, adorned the kitchen area. A large double bed lay against the northern portion of the circular wall. The center of the building was their living room, and in typical Fijian style, there was no bathroom, only an outhouse.

On our way back to Viani Bay, Rog talked with Jack about our need to locate safe cyclone holes for *Dreamer*. Without a safe haven in which to hide our boat, the odds of *Dreamer* surviving a cyclone would be small, and we had no insurance on our boat. Insurance was only obtainable if an overseas vessel was crewed by at least three people, and we had no intention of having extra people on board for any longer than a two-to-three week visit. But if we lost our boat in a cyclone, we would lose at least half of everything we owned at that point in our lives.

Finding a cyclone hole created another day of togetherness as Jack and Sofi, Rik and Ann, and Rog and I set out to explore a location several hours to the west. On the trip there, Sofi and I sang while Jack and Rik tended a two-hundred pound test line with a Rebel-style fishing lure that was extended off of *Dreamer's* stern. Jack promised us that should a cyclone threaten Fiji, he and Abu, together with his brother-in-law and at least one of his five brothers would help haul our yacht up into the mucky backwaters of the mangroves located about one-quarter of the way between Viani Bay and Savusavu.

Upon investigation of this area, called Fawn Harbour, we determined that if a cyclone approached from the east, *Dreamer* would indeed be safe and survive the strong winds, especially since there would be little surge-back amongst the many mangrove trees. We had already located another safe haven for *Dreamer* should a cyclone threaten from the west. It turned out that Fiji was not threatened at all by a cyclone during the 1995-96 season, but determining what we would do in case there was one gave us peace of mind.

On the trip home, Jack and Rik caught five walus. This white meat fish was a favorite of the Fijians and at three feet each, could feed many villagers. After filleting and deboning each fish, Jack offered one to Rik and Ann and one to Rog and me, which we gladly accepted.

Legacy arrived the next day. There was much hugging and chatting and dining as we welcomed Paul and Dianne Holmes from Nelson into our midst. I loved hearing the Kiwi accent of these native New Zealanders. This amazing couple had spent ten years building *Legacy* in their spare time, when they weren't working or raising their two daughters. It was exciting to hear their version of the various experiences they'd had since leaving New Zealand in June on *Legacy's* maiden voyage.

One of my own favorite adventures took place the next day. It was a normal Taveuni shopping day. I had talked Jack into leaving a tad earlier than usual so that Sofi and I could visit Bouma National Heritage Park, located near the northeastern shore of Taveuni Island. I had read about Bouma Falls and Sofi told me she'd never seen them. I was determined to pack her life with as much enjoyment as possible while Rog and I were in the neighborhood, so although Jack and Rog weren't interested, I invited our four yachtie friends to come along. Rik and Ann declined, explaining that they needed to do some boat work before *Romper's* and *Legacy's* departure for northwestern Fiji, but Dianne and Paul were enthusiastic about joining Sofi and me.

The day of our trip, I dressed in accordance with Fijian custom. I felt a bit like Little Bo Peep in my purple and turquoise sarong with purple T-shirt, a big white hat for protection from the tropical sun, the walking stick I had acquired before hiking the Milford Track in New Zealand and Tevas on my feet. I also carried a daypack stuffed with camera gear, food and a bathing suit. Sofi looked cool and comfortable in a long, loose, black-and-white patterned top that covered her red pants down to the knees. Although she chose to wear no shoes, for this special occasion Sofi allowed her thick, black curly hair to fall naturally down to her shoulders, resembling a long black Afro. Dianne was practical in a short denim skirt and loose yellow T-shirt that complimented her shoulder-length, straight auburn hair and dancing brown eyes.

As we approached the falls, a fragrant mist filled the air. The Bouma Falls are located within luxuriant foliage, accented by stands of wild ginger with their brilliant red, cone-shaped blossoms. Tons of water cascaded seventy-two feet down a rock wall into a large, deep pool of water. The marvel of Bouma Falls is that there is not just one waterfall or even two, but three sets at different elevations, connected by a hiking trail that weaves its way up the mountain through extremely lush vegetation and across several streams.

The four of us gawked at the incredible beauty surrounding us everywhere in this Fijian Shangri-La. Sofi darted ahead up the trail and I called out, "Hey Sofi, I thought you'd never been here before!" She laughed with glee and sped upward and across a stream, amused to see the three *vavalangis* tentatively trying to keep our balance on the smooth rocks as we crossed over to her side.

When we reached the second falls, I ducked behind some vegetation, unzipped my backpack and quickly changed into my bathing suit. Sofi and I joyously jumped into the chilly pool at the base of these falls and played in the water, dunking, splashing and swimming together for at least half an hour while Dianne and Paul ate lunch. I was grateful that Paul took several treasured photos of Sofi and me having so much fun in the pool. Sofi was afraid to swim right under the falls but I enjoyed showing off, with the falls pounding down on top of my head.

Changing back into our clothes, we quickly ate our lunch and proceeded to the third falls. Looking down from the edge of the trail near these top falls, we saw a profusion of deep green fertility with only a tiny ribbon of trail visible in one small open area far below. Finally we headed back down the mountain, managing to catch the proper bus back to Waiyevo where Jack and the rest of the Viani Bay shoppers were waiting to head home on the *I Loi*.

The next day, all six *vavalangis* boarded *Romper* and *Legacy*, and towing *Gos* behind *Romper*, we set out for Vodovodonabolo Bay. Rog and I wanted to give our yachtie friends an opportunity to experience this beautiful cove and perhaps meet Glory, although I figured the odds were against it. We arrived shortly before lunchtime to find an unusual light drizzle falling from an overcast, gray sky. This didn't keep us from snorkeling though, and I was amazed by the unusually vast array of marine life we observed. Afterwards, sitting in *Romper's* cockpit enjoying lunch, Ann explained that the gray skies confused the fish, leaving them unsure whether it was daytime or nighttime. Hence both the daytime feeders and the nighttime feeders *all* emerged from their underwater dens to dine on the coral reefs.

After lunch I walked forward onto *Romper's* bow and although I could hardly believe my eyes, I was sure I spied Glory. Excited beyond words, I urged Ann to accompany me back into the water to experience Glory, but she was less than enthusiastic. Perhaps her mind was occupied with thoughts of leaving this area and moving on? In any case, I didn't hold it against her.

We bid them bon voyage as we boarded *Gos* and headed back to Viani Bay, leaving them alone in Vodovodonabolo Bay for another thirty-six hours before their planned departure. Rog and I honestly hoped that we would reconnect with Paul and Dianne as well as Rik and Ann at some future time and place.

Before we knew it, Fiji Day was upon us. Sixteen Fijian youngsters ranging from four to thirteen scrambled aboard *Dreamer*. Sofi brought aboard two woven baskets filled with Fijian delicacies including breadfruit, fried bananas, yams and chicken wrapped in banana leaves, all ready for baking in a small *lovo* oven that she would create on the beach.

Rog and I were thrilled to have the young ones on board. Their excitement was contagious and Loi looked proud as she showed her friends around our boat. It took a while to untangle our anchor from the coral heads fifty feet below *Dreamer*. When we finally got underway, we needed our engine since the wind was nonexistent during the morning hours. Jack, Andrea and Abu went ahead of us on the *I Loi* with more supplies. As we rounded the reef and headed into Vodovodonabolo Bay, my excitement grew at the prospect of possibly seeing Glory again. My hopes were high since she was still alive and well several days earlier.

I had only once seen another giant triggerfish in Vodovodonabolo Bay and that was the fish I referred to as Glory's mate. During the seven-and-a-half years Rog and I dove in tropical waters, we never saw or heard of a giant triggerfish behaving like Glory. The others have either ignored human beings or hid from them. I was convinced beyond a shadow of a doubt that the fish we'd seen a few days before was Glory. Additionally, while most yellowmargin giant triggerfish have a blue stripe adjacent to their bold golden-yellow stripe, Glory's accent stripe was black.

As always when approaching an anchorage, I climbed up the mast steps to ensure that *Dreamer's* submerged keel would not collide with any bommies below the surface. Rog navigated *Dreamer* into much shallower water for our one-day picnic than where we had previously anchored. Soon the anchor was set and the older children quickly dove into the water, heading for the beach sixty feet away. Sofi herded the younger ones into our dinghy and Rog ferried them ashore.

The *I Loi* was already anchored about three boat lengths off of *Dreamer's* port side. I heard Andrea calling out to me that Glory was swimming near the *I Loi* and I almost jumped in the water immediately, but stopped long enough to put on my mask and snorkel before making haste to the *I Loi*. When I was within three yards of Andrea, she began throwing bread chunks toward me, the closest of which landed on the surface only about fifteen inches from where I was treading water, and Glory swam right over to grab them. She was so close to me, the closest she had ever come.

In that clear, shallow water, only about seventeen feet deep, the sunlight reflecting up from the bottom and down from the sky made Glory's colors the most brilliant I had yet seen. The white sandy bottom created a stark contrast for the vividly colored blue-green diamonds covering most of her fifteen-inch length. Glory and I swam around the *I Loi* together for a while as Andrea and Abu looked on, mesmerized, until a tall Fijian lad from Taveuni made a sudden dive down towards Glory and scared her off.

I hadn't noticed a third boat was now anchored in the cove, but Andrea told me that Loi's schoolmates on Taveuni Island had gotten wind of the picnic and came over to play volleyball and share the day with us. I swam ashore to watch the kids play volleyball for a while. Loi was undoubtedly the star player, jumping higher than the others to hammer the ball across the net with alarming accuracy. She actually outplayed all of the boys, not to mention the other girls.

Something was bothering me as I sat watching the kids playing volleyball, and I finally figured out what it was —Abu's enthrallment with Glory. I glanced over towards the *I Loi,* and behold, the little boat was gone. Had he gone back to Viani Bay for his spear gun? I suddenly feared for Glory's survival, but there was nothing I could do about it at that moment.

Appetites ignited as the aroma of baked chicken and yams wafted into the air from Sofi's *lovo.* Rog chauffeured Sofi and me back to *Dreamer* to collect the remainder of the food from our refrigerator and to my utter delight, there was Glory, swimming around our stern. I was so happy! A few young children were hanging onto an inner tube nearby and when they were close enough to hear me, I said softly, "Girls, there's a very special fish right over here behind the boat." They paddled quietly in the direction I'd indicated and were soon close enough to see Glory. I was amazed at their respect for her. Glory must have sensed this because they didn't scare her away; however she didn't come especially close to the surface, either, so it was difficult for Sofi to get a good look at her.

"Mrs. Debby, is that Glory?" a child asked me quietly.

"Yes, darling, it is. Isn't she just wonderful?" They agreed that she was and paddled off towards the beach. I simply could not stifle my natural inclination to share something as wonderful as Glory, despite my concerns about Abu. When we left for the beach, laden with several large canvas carrying bags, Glory was out of sight.

The most remarkable thing about lunch was the obedient behavior of all the children, including the teenagers. When served, most of the kids gobbled up their food immediately. Sofi told them they had to wait until everyone else had been served before they took any seconds, and each child obeyed without complaint. We had observed this behavior throughout Fiji and most of the other island nations we visited as well. Children showed respect not only for their own parents, but for all other adults. There was no back talk, whining or complaining and while they were often filled with joy and sometimes even mischievousness, they were politely obedient and did not have to be told twice how to behave. At the end of the day, back aboard *Dreamer*, Sofi announced that the kids could not go below because they were all either wet or sandy. Once again, there were no arguments or complaints. Everyone simply stayed topside.

Abu and Andrea finally reappeared in the *I Loi* to pick up Jack. Apparently they had been off romancing in solitude for a couple of precious hours. I was relieved that my fear had been unfounded, and Abu hadn't disappeared to retrieve his spear gun.

The serene weather that helped to make our picnic special again prevented us from sailing back into Viani Bay, so we powered all the way. When Jack came over to *Dreamer* with a small outboard to pick up the children, I grabbed our camera and took a treasured shot of the departing youngsters as they were all waving good-bye.

That night, I had a brilliant idea. "You know, Rog, Sofi didn't really get a good look at Glory today, and besides, I don't have a single underwater photo of Glory. I'm thinking of inviting Sofi to go back to Vodovodonabolo Bay with me tomorrow in *Gos*. I'll take our underwater camera and some bread. Do you have any objection to that plan?"

"No, but be careful."

"Of course."

"That way, with you two off on another adventure, I can get some rest! In fact, can we skip dinner and go to bed?"

"Sounds good to me, m'darlin'. Love you."

"Love you, too."

Chapter 11

PORTRAIT SESSION AND NET FISHING

Because the hot tropical sun makes exercising uncomfortable, I made a habit of arising before dawn to begin my forty-minute exercise routine on the foredeck. Sofi also arose early to accomplish as much *caka caka*, or work, as she could before the heat of the day. So it was that bright and early on the morning after Fiji Day, I heard Sofi whistling and calling my name from the beach. She held the fresh cow's milk I had ordered from one of her neighbors two days previously, so I boarded *Gos* and went to shore to retrieve it from her. I told Sofi about my plan to photograph Glory and she was most enthusiastic. I also invited her and Jack for dinner, asking her to invite Andrea and Abu as well. Jack's mother, May, was now too old to get in and out of boats or I definitely would have invited her.

I did my exercises on *Dreamer's* bow, went below deck to meditate in privacy, and then gathered together masks, snorkels and fins for both Sofi and me. I threw together a simple lunch and stored it in the refrigerator, together with four chicken breasts I had extracted from our freezer for dinner. Next I worked on the underwater camera, re-greasing the three O-rings and inserting a brand new roll of 100 ASA, 36-exposure slide film. Then I woke Rog and began preparing breakfast, after which I got out my *On Deck Log* and wrote about our adventures thus far in Viani Bay, until it was time to go ashore and pick up Sofi.

Throwing all of our equipment and lunch, plus some drinking water, into *Gos*, I headed for the beach. Of course, my darling friend was waiting there, eager to jump aboard. Off we sped, feeling like two truants playing hooky from school. We smiled at each other with love in our hearts as the slightly choppy water sent an occasional spray into the boat.

Once we rounded the reef and turned into Vodovodonabolo Bay, the water was calm and flat. I decided to anchor *Gos* in the approximate location of *Dreamer's* original anchorage. The water was fairly deep here, and in retrospect I realized that I should have gone into the shallower water where the sun's rays penetrated through to the white sandy bottom, giving a better backdrop for Glory's portrait session. However, I wanted to be sure that Glory would come to us and she did so without hesitation.

Eager to record this incredibly friendly fish on film, I was the first to go into the water with her. Glory was so accustomed to swimming with me that it was easy to get half a dozen decent shots of her, although I chose not to use any flash for fear of spooking her.

When it was Sofi's turn, I realized that she was not accustomed to wearing a mask, so I used spittle on the lens to decrease the possibility that it would fog up on her. I carefully smoothed her tight black curls away from her face and asked her to hold them back as I placed the mask over her head and pulled the strap tighter so that it would fit securely against her head. As she placed the snorkel into her mouth, I explained that she must breathe both in and out through her mouth. She practiced this before slithering over the rounded rubber sides of *Gos* and into the water.

I watched for Glory but when she didn't surface for a couple of minutes, I threw some bread chunks into the water near Sofi. Glory was quick to respond. I watched Sofi and Glory enjoying each other and couldn't wait to hear what Sofi had to say about the experience. Finally, after almost twenty minutes, Sofi swam over to *Gos* and I helped her aboard.

As I removed the mask, I couldn't contain myself. "How was it, Sofi?"

"Wow, I swim with a fish! And she beautiful, wonderful! I feel very happy." This is what I wanted to hear from my dear friend. I felt certain that if English had been her primary language, she would have shared more of her feelings of elation with me but I accepted her brief answer, coupled with the excited look on her face and her animated body language as ample proof that she was over the top, just as I always felt after swimming with Glory.

Even though she was no longer in sight, we said good-bye to Glory as we pulled up the small anchor and putt-putted ashore to harvest lemons for iced tea and coconut husks to fuel the cooking stove. We relaxed on the pristine sand, enjoying our corned beef and mustard sandwiches as we drank in the solitude and intense beauty that was Vodovodonabolo Bay.

"Sofi," I said, "You seemed very quiet whenever we were with Rik and Ann. You weren't your usual happy self. Didn't you like them?"

"*Sega na leqa,*" she replied. "*Meda marau.*"

With these Fijian phrases, meaning no worries and be happy, she dropped the conversation. I suppose she was correct to dismiss my concerns. After all, Ann and Rik were gone now and if Sofi was a little bit jealous of my history and friendship with Ann, as I suspected, the past was the past and no longer mattered to her. I felt that the Fijians did a better job of staying in the present moment, not worrying about the past or the future, than I did. Perhaps I could learn something from this!

Changing the subject, I asked Sofi if she'd like to stop inside Viani Bay on the way home to snorkel the reef just south of Yanuyanu Island, explaining that with a mask she'd be able to see the beauty of the coral and the small reef fish, and the flippers would let her swim just by kicking her feet. She wouldn't have to use her arms.

"Yes, I want to try," she replied.

Once outside the protected waters of the smaller Vodovodonabolo Bay, the water was still choppy. I hoped Sofi would not take any water into her mouth through the top of the snorkel. When we approached the reef, I set the anchor, then outfitted Sofi in mask, snorkel and fins. I told her how to blow air forcefully out of her mouth if any water came into her snorkel.

Immediately after entering the water, we successfully swam the short distance to the reef. I stayed right by Sofi's side and began pointing at beautiful fish and pieces of coral for her to look at. However, when I looked over at her, she appeared apprehensive, so I motioned for her to stand on the reef. Sofi knew about sea urchins and was careful not to put her finned foot down on one of them. When I stood up, I could feel how swiftly the water was moving over the top of the reef as the tide moved in, making it even choppier than the deeper water. I asked Sofi whether any water had come into her snorkel and she said no, but a little water had seeped into the side of the mask. We took it off, emptied and reset it, all while Sofi was clinging to my arm.

"Listen, Sofi, let's swim back to *Gos* and maybe we'll try this again some time when the water is calmer. What do you think?" She nodded and though she still looked scared, she also seemed relieved.

We started out towards *Gos* with Sofi clinging to my arm but soon she had instinctively positioned herself so that a portion of her body weight was on top of my back. I asked God to help me keep afloat with Sofi halfway across my back, and with that divine assistance, we made it safely back to the small boat. Sofi scrambled aboard rapidly with the help of my boosting thrust on the bottom of her flippers. Once aboard, I threw a towel around her shivering form, waiting for her to collect herself. I didn't want to take her home still feeling frightened so I reminded her of her successful swim earlier with Glory. That memory seemed to reassure her, so I started the engine, hoisted the small anchor and took Sofi back to the beach at the foot of the hill leading to the Homestead.

"Don't forget about dinner," I told her, reminding her to bring Andrea and Abu along too.

That evening, the four of them arrived in the *I Loi*. I handed up into the cockpit four glasses of iced tea and a platter of cheese and crackers. Not long afterwards, I asked Andrea if she would come below and show me how to make the chicken curry stir fry she'd created for May's birthday.

The brown rice was already cooking and I had previously cut up the four chicken breasts into approximately three-quarter-inch chunks. The tall, elegant woman was in her element as she explained each step to me. In the tropics, they grow small squash that look like mini-pumpkins, only sometimes they are gray and sometimes they are dark green. We took one of these from *Dreamer's* vegetable net, cut it in half, deseeded it, then peeled, cubed and boiled it till tender and drained it. We sliced a medium-sized onion, minced four large cloves of garlic and an inch-and-a-half section of peeled, fresh ginger. Finally, we chopped up a green pepper.

Next we melted three tablespoons of butter in a fry pan, added a dollop of safflower oil and a bit of salt. When hot, we added the onion, garlic, ginger and green pepper. As these vegetables were sautéing, Andrea added about two teaspoons of curry spice, explaining that you had to add enough so that "it looks right."

After the vegetables cooked three or four minutes, we added the chicken and some salt and stir-fried everything another three minutes, before lowering the heat and covering the pan. After another three minutes we added the pumpkin, stirred it again, returned the lid and let the whole thing cook another two minutes or so.

Andrea tested the chicken by cutting a piece to make sure it was white all the way through. Next she portioned out the brown rice onto six plates, served the chicken curry and vegetables alongside the rice, then squeezed the juice from a half lemon over the individual servings. She explained that in this dish, the curry blends with the other flavors rather than predominating.

"It sure smells good down here," Jack said as he made his way down the companionway ladder. Sofi slid in and around to the far side of our table in the main salon.

"Thanks, Jack. I hope it's as good as it smells, but you know that this is Andrea's creation, not mine!" Andrea beamed gratefully at the recognition. Everyone dove in and there was a period of silence as we devoured the meal.

"Say," Abu piped up as Andrea and I got in each other's way clearing the dishes off the table, "how is it that you swim with a wild fish? I mean how did it happen in the first place? You know that we Fijians spear and eat these *cumudamu*, so it's really surprising that one of them is actually swimming with a human."

"Well, Abu," I replied, "I've been asking myself that same question, and here's the only thing I've come up with so far. I've spent a lot of years now seeking a direct personal experience with God. I have always recognized the presence of God in the beauty of Nature, but I've hungered for an experience where I actually felt like God cares about me. I've been aware several times during this voyage when God has been protecting Rog and me and *Dreamer*, but I still had this empty feeling inside of me that I knew could only be filled by an assurance of God's love for me. Now I'm beginning to feel more assured of that great love since Glory has been surfacing alongside *Dreamer* and *Gos* without fail every single time I've come into Vodovodonabolo Bay.

"I honestly believe that God is directing this beautiful fish to befriend me as a sign to show me that She has heard my prayers, that She is always here for me, and that She loves me unconditionally. I feel like a changed person: divinely loved; completely fulfilled; protected, heard and personally cared for by God."

Silence ensued as awe appeared on all the faces around the table, including my own, I was sure. I had not come to such specific conclusions before and I was sure that God had just flowed through me as I shared this sudden inner realization.

After some moments passed, Jack asked me, "Would you like to go net fishing with us tomorrow morning?" I was more than a little bit surprised at this invitation and finally responded, "I know that you and your family have to eat and I just ate the flesh of a chicken that used to be alive. I tried a vegetarian diet for seven years but suffered from hypoglycemia. My doctor told me I had to eat one portion of animal protein every day. I'm healthy now, but I still hate killing and eating any living being, so no, I don't want to go net fishing with you tomorrow morning. Thanks for asking anyway."

"We'd really like you to come with us, wouldn't we, Sofi?" Jack responded. Sofi nodded yes and Jack knew he had me hooked. I always took advantage of every opportunity to spend time with my hard-working friend. Sofi and I had bonded instantly from the moment we met a year earlier, perhaps because our friendship gave me the opportunity to be a big sister again, so many miles away from my actual three younger sisters. But it was also Sofi's endearing, impish qualities, combined with her work ethic that caused me to love her so. In truth, she was young enough to be the daughter I never had. Also, she was so tiny and yet so flamboyant and energetic that I was instantly drawn to her, just as Jack must have been when he first met her in Raviravi Village.

The next morning I was in *Dreamer's* cockpit watching Abu and Jack load the long fishing net with affixed floats onto the wooden skiff that would be towed behind the *I Loi*. Sofi hopped into the *I Loi* with a basket laden with what I presumed to be food, and Jack also put a large bucket aboard to contain the captured fish. Two fourteen-year-old boys, Semisi and Abel, also got aboard together with Sesel, Jr., who might have been about ten. The sun was up, fairly low in the eastern sky, and a rarely seen group of wild horses were wading in the shallow water near the head of the bay.

From the fire-operated ovens on shore wafted the scent of cinnamon from baked scones, and I suspected that Sofi had a dozen or more of those tasty morsels in her woven basket. She wore an ankle-length sarong wrapped around her waist. The length of sarongs can be easily adjusted simply by rolling up the top to create whatever length is wanted before tying the two ends together around the waist. I also had a sarong tied around my waist but underneath mine was a Western-style, one-piece bathing suit, something that no Fijian woman I ever met possessed. They simply went into the water in their sarongs or in lightweight cotton pants like Sofi wore the day we photographed Glory.

I was not a bit surprised when Sofi distributed scones to all on board and then passed around a knife and the blackberry jam. Warm and delicious, that scone seemed to melt in my mouth. However, I *was* surprised and actually alarmed when the *I Loi* began putt-putting into Vodovodonabolo Bay! "Why Jack, you're not going to fish *here*, are you?"

"Yes we are and that's why we invited you along. We want you to fish-sit Glory so she won't get caught in our net." No other words could cause the relief I felt in my heart. When looking into Abu's eyes, I could see an affirmation there that assured me he would never intentionally harm my beloved pet fish, God's symbol of Her love for me and for all of Her children.

I was close to tears of gratitude as Jack anchored the *I Loi* near the same location he'd chosen on Fiji Day. Sure enough, Glory arrived on the scene only minutes later. Leaving my sarong and T-shirt behind, I quietly entered the water in my bathing suit, using Abu's mask and snorkel. Doing the breaststroke and the frog kick, I swam with Glory away from the *I Loi*. Abu was already pulling up the anchor, and the Fijians were soon putt-putting over to the other side of the bay.

Glory and I swam together for a fairly long time, perhaps half an hour. She was swimming very close to me in that bright, shallow water. I decided to try a new routine with her. She'd be about a meter or two ahead of me when I'd pause, dive straight down to the bottom, which was only about fifteen feet; then I'd turn away in the opposite direction from where she was swimming and in no time at all, I'd see her swimming parallel to me and only about two arm-lengths away. I purposefully did my dive when she was ahead of me, then swam away from her to give her the choice of either turning around to catch up with me or not. I did this several times and she really seemed to like it. I sure did!

Even before I saw it, I heard the sound of large outboard motors and looked up to see one of the Rainbow Reef commercial dive boats coming into the bay for an early picnic lunch break. Glory scooted off and I made for the beach before the boat had a chance to anchor. I knew all three of the Fijian dive masters on board and they invited me to join them for lunch. Their English was good, so I chatted with them and their customers about their morning dives.

After the dive boat left, I swam out into the bay looking for Glory. She was nowhere to be found so I returned to the beach and waited for the *I Loi* to return. Lying on the beach and gazing into the deep blue sky, I thanked God with all of my heart for the abundant blessings She was constantly bestowing upon me. I was certain, now, that I would never again feel emptiness inside me because I was beginning to feel that sense of Oneness, a sense that the same Consciousness and Energy that animated Glory and all of Creation was also animating me! I had always been blessed with material abundance and with people who loved me, but having this direct experience of God's existence right within me was what my soul had been hankering for all these years.

After the return of the intrepid fisher-people, I asked Semisi and Abel whether they would like to swim out to Glory's bommie with me to look for her, and they nodded yes. But just as we reached her bommie, Jack called to us that Glory was over next to the boat. We swam back quickly and I stayed right by the side of the *I Loi* to encourage the boys to swim with her. But apparently, according to Jack who could see from above, they had already scared her off. Semisi and Abel climbed up on the *I Loi* and left me in the water, hopefully to swim with Glory again.

Sofi had one scone left. I wouldn't be surprised had she told me that she had reserved it especially for this occasion. She broke off a piece of it and tossed it into the water within fifteen inches of my body, and sure enough, Glory appeared from *somewhere* to get it.

Now we were on a roll again, enjoying being together. She was swimming quite close to me. I repeated my dive-down-to-the-bottom trick a couple of times and again, Glory turned around and swam parallel to me, right near the white sandy bottom. When I finally said a mental good-bye to Glory and re-boarded the boat, Jack was beaming from ear to ear. After we got going, he kept exclaiming over and over again about how close Glory came to me, how used to me she had become and how wonderful it was that I had a pet fish. He even said he wished that he had one. I replied that it truly was wonderful.

Chapter 12

GLOOM FILLS VIANI BAY

In late October, the unthinkable happened to the residents of Viani Bay. One morning Ed Fisher simply did not wake up. His wife, Aseta, was devastated and the villagers went into a month-long period of grieving, celebrating Ed's life and comforting Aseta. We were in Viani Bay the previous year when Sukuna, the twenty-seven-year-old adopted son of Jack's brother Chris Fisher, was killed by a shark while spearfishing. Sukuna's funeral was traumatic enough, but this was different.

Boats from all over Fiji filled the large bay day after day, laden with food and the people who knew Ed for his purity of heart and his years of ministry. When we paid our respects to Aseta, she wept openly. "If I had only known he was going to leave us, I would have asked his forgiveness for all the times I was critical of him," she cried. Holding her head to my chest, I tried to assure her that Ed was even now looking down upon her and forgiving her for any wrongs she might have committed.

"Aseta, we are all human so please don't worry about the past. Ed is with God in heaven right now. His love for you has not changed and I'm sure he understands that we are all fallible human beings. He forgives you." I cradled her head until she stopped weeping.

For ten days, we stayed on board *Dreamer* and watched the boats come and go. Occasionally Jack would stop by just long enough to drop off a couple of lobsters or other delicacies. We'd thank him, ask how Aseta was doing, and then he'd be on his way. Being the custodian of the Fisher Homestead, he had many host responsibilities and we could only imagine how busy Sofi must be with all the visitors. We never saw her during this period.

Finally one afternoon we told Jack that we planned to visit Matagi and Qamea Islands for a while and asked him to give our love to Aseta and Sofi. After assuring Jack we'd return before Christmas, each of us received a big bear hug from this large affectionate man. We raised our anchor and wound our way through the visiting crafts until we reached Somosomo Strait. As we passed the entrance to Vodovodonabolo Bay, I blew a kiss and sent lots of love to Glory. I prayed she would still be there when we returned.

Matagi Island is an ancient sunken volcano with a wide opening on the north side. Like Vodovodonabolo Bay, no one lives in this northern bay except for fish that feed on the coral heads and coral fringes close to the shore, the many birds that fill the air with their chatter, and some wild pigs that eat roots and dig around in the sand. After engaging in highly social activity during the past few months, we were ready for a respite in yet another secluded Shangri-La.

After setting our anchor, the first thing we did was dive into the gorgeous clear blue water to check out the marine life around the coral. We could see from the surface that our anchor was set securely and our fathometer registered a depth of forty feet. The second thing we did was to install our woven hammock between our headstay and the mast.

As much as we loved the dear souls who live in Viani Bay, we relished our privacy and lingered over a dinner of barbecued yellow-fin tuna, boiled Fijian spinach and fried eggplant. Chatting in the cockpit was a treat as the sun sank behind the western rim of the old volcano. I brought out my guitar to strum and sing a few songs. Before long, Rog and I were in each other's arms and our passion mounted quickly as we caressed, stroked and kissed each other in our most sensitive areas. *Dreamer* seemed to rock to our natural rhythm as our bodies moved together, moaning in delight until that ecstatic release. The after-shocks I experienced were particularly sweet as we lay in each other's arms afterwards in contentment, heat and quiet joy.

When I awoke in the wee hours of the morning, I went on deck to find the stars reaching down to greet and welcome me with their twinkling luminosity. No city lights impeded my reverie. And so the days passed; two days, four days, walks on the island, reading in the hammock, six days, a week, long meditations, two weeks, banana nut bread and sourdough banana pancakes, three weeks.

We spent Thanksgiving at the Qamea Beach Club, located on a nearby island, with "Papa Peter" Sutter and his partner, Christina, who together plied the Fijian waters for many a year on Peter's sailboat, *Wild Spirit*. Jo Kloss, a personal friend of Peter's from their days in Sausalito, was kind enough to treat all four of us to a traditional American Thanksgiving dinner. We felt privileged to be included in this gathering. Peter had cancer and the local Fijians who lived in nearby Naiviivi Bay knew that this would be his last visit to their village. They honored him with hand-woven mats and gave hand-woven purses to Christina and me. On the morning of Peter's departure, they all gathered down by the water in front of the Qamea Beach Club and sang the beautiful "Fijian Farewell Song" to him and Christina.

We retreated to Matagi with thoughts of Peter and Christina, Jo, and the Fijians of Qamea Island in our hearts. I composed a newsletter that I hoped would be mailed from Taveuni Island before Christmas. I learned new songs on the guitar and spent a morning observing and quietly swimming near a school of dolphins that were circling in their sleep state. After long morning meditations, I cooled off with dips into the crystal clear water as the daytime temperatures reached increasingly higher numbers.

We got to know the Fijian crew members of the dive boat *Matagi Princess II*. Although the Matagi resort was on the southwestern side of Matagi Island, the crew of the dive boat was aware that *Dreamer* was anchored in the northern bay. Whenever the dive boat had no paying passengers, the crew came around to "our" bay to give us fresh produce in exchange for borrowing VHS movie tapes to watch on the *Matagi Princess II*.

In this way, we got to know these interesting young Fijian men and received enough produce to keep us well supplied. They also told us about the best walking trails on the island and took us to uninhabited Motualevu where we dove the most gorgeous vertical wall we'd ever experienced. The vertical drop was well over two hundred feet, the visibility was perfect, the sea life and soft corals abundant.

I had occasional flashes of missing Glory during our idyllic time on Matagi and by the second week in December, thoughts about the people of Viani Bay were crowding into my brain. I knew it was time for us to return to our friends, so on the morning of December 14th, we weighed anchor and headed west once more. By 8:10 a.m. we were in open waters where we set the mainsail and unfurled the genoa. With a flood tide behind us, we covered the thirty nautical miles back to Viani Bay in no time and dropped our anchor in our customary location, just offshore from the Fisher Homestead.

Immediately, my intuition told me that things were somehow different. The very air felt heavy and no one came down to the beach or out to *Dreamer* to welcome us. This was very unusual. In fact, I didn't see anyone.

"Rog, what do you think has happened here?"

"I don't know," he replied.

"Well, let's go ashore and see if anyone is around."

We motored the short distance to shore and still no sight nor sound of anyone. As we approached the house, we heard a diminished version of Sofi's typically excited voice calling out to us from the direction of the pigpen.

"Sofi, where is everyone?" I asked as I gave her a big hug.

"Oh, Debby, very bad since you left! May sign papers and Jack *not* going to get Homestead after she die. He very angry when he find out and leave to sail for Australia on Australian boat, *Galaxy*. Boat in Savusavu right now and leave for Australia at end of January."

"I don't believe it. What are you going to do?"

"What can I do? Loi and I still living in big house with May and Raua and Andrea. No problem now with May alive, but she get chill attacks sometimes because of bad malaria she got long ago. If she die, big problem. I tell Jack I wait here till he come back."

"But when will that be?"

"That is problem," she said mournfully, now beginning to sob. "I don't know if he ever come back."

"Of course he will."

"Well, I don't know. He really mad because he here all these years for May and house and grounds and animals, since father die, and now no Homestead for him after May die. Where we live if he do come back? Jack so mad he never live in house again."

"Sofi, you can always build your own house. Jack helped Phil and Tamara build their *bure*, so surely he can build a house for you and Loi. I'm sure that many of your friends would help you."

"I don't know. He say he write to me and maybe send for me when he get to Australia . . ."

My heart went out to this normally energetic, animated woman who now looked slumped and dejected. Jack was such a presence that the very air in Viani Bay felt different without him.

"Sofi, let me think about things. Maybe there is something we can do for you. Will Jack come home for Christmas?"

"Never," Sofi replied emphatically.

"Okay. We have some time between now and the end of January. Is Abu still around?"

"Yes. Jack tell him to take people over to Taveuni in *I Loi* to shop. Abu and Andrea keep all of money from trips but supposed to give some of money to me for Loi's school on Taveuni."

I put my arms around her small frame, and she began to cry on my shoulder. "It's okay. Everything is going to work out. You'll see. God will not abandon you and things almost always have a way of turning out for the best. But you have to believe that and have faith."

"You think so?"

"I do. Now when is Abu making his next trip to Taveuni? We need lots of stuff."

"In three days because he go yesterday," Sofi said. "You want I bring you something?"

"Some eggplants and string beans and pawpaw would be great."

"The big mango tree full, so we go there now and get lots for you."

"Okay, let's do it."

The huge tree was just to the west side of the house and when May saw us approaching she came out onto the porch to welcome us. I ran up the steps to give her a big hug.

"Welcome back," she said, giving us her typical half smile.

I couldn't hold back from exclaiming, "Oh May, don't you miss Jack?"

"Yes I do." I was sure I might see a tear, but the matriarch of the family remained stoic. She reminded me a little bit of Queen Elizabeth. She knew she had a job to do, that of preserving the land that surrounded Viani Bay for the future of the Fisher family, and she wasn't going to let her emotions stand in the way of her duty.

"You stay for Christmas?" she asked, changing the subject.

"We're planning to do that," Rog said.

"Good. Debby can play Christmas carols on guitar for children when they decorate tree on December 20. Sara Fisher celebrating twenty-first birthday on December 23 with very big party on lawn. Maybe one hundred people come. Can you take pictures for family? Can you do these things?"

"May, I'll be happy to," I said.

"Good. You come and play sweep with Andrea, Sofi and me. We not have good card game since Jack leave. Sofi can make scones and some iced tea. You come tomorrow? And Roger, you come too."

"Thank you," Rog said. "And by the way, how is Aseta doing?"

"She very sad, especially because people not come anymore since end of November. Little Eddie and family stay on at Yanuyanu Island, so good company for her."

"That's good," Roger replied. "We'll want to go visit her sometime."

"Mom, you have bowl or basket for Debby and Roger to take mangos back to *Dreamer*?" Sofi asked.

"Of course," May said as she disappeared into the house. A minute later May's maid, Raua, returned with a hand-woven basket which Sofi, Rog and I loaded up with mangos. Sofi said she would have some eggplants, beans and pawpaws ready for us tomorrow when we came to play cards.

That evening Rog and I discussed Sofi's plight and what we might be able to do to help.

"I've been thinking, honey," Rog said, "we might consider buying a larger inflatable that will make it easier for us to load and unload our scuba equipment. We can't use *Gos* to take Buddy and Ruth diving when they come in March because our dinghy is too small."

"That's an interesting idea, but I really wanted to talk about how we can help Sofi."

"There's a correlation," Rog replied. "If we have a new dinghy shipped here from New Zealand, we could have it sent directly to Savusavu, and that's where Jack is until the end of January, right?"

I almost knocked down the table rushing over to give Rog a long, drawn out kiss. "You are brilliant," I exclaimed after coming up for air. "You are saying that we could order the dinghy and then take Sofi with us when we go to pick it up."

"Yep, that's the idea. We can take Loi, too, if that would work better for Sofi, or leave her in school."

"Perfect. Now the only question is whether we can afford a new dinghy. Have you done any research? How much will this set us back? Will we need a new engine or will our eight horsepower Evinrude work? What will we do with *Gos*? And who will you order from? I haven't exactly seen a bunch of catalogues on board *Dreamer* lately."

"Slow down a minute, girl! I had a long discussion with Peter Sutter at the Qamea Beach Club while you and

Christina were playing dominos, and Jo let us use her computer to do some research. There's a great company in Auckland that makes inflatables of all types, and we can take delivery within two months of placing an order. We're probably also going to have to purchase a larger outboard motor to power the size dinghy we'll want, but I'm pretty sure we can buy a new fifteen horsepower Mercury in Savusavu. Off the top of my head, I'm not sure what the exact cost will be for these two purchases, but I printed out some information at the Beach Club and I'll take a look at those papers later tonight. As for *Gos*, I'm certain that we'll find a good home for her and the Evinrude, although I doubt we'll get much money for either one of them."

"Well, you sneaky little rascal. You and Peter had this all planned out, and you didn't say a word to me about it at Matagi."

"I was just waiting for the right time, m'darlin'."

"Getting back to Sofi," I said. "I have no intention of waiting to tell her about this plan! We'll have to place this order soon if we're going to get her to Savusavu on time."

"We can place the order when we go to Taveuni with Abu on the 17th. And we can always leave for Savusavu before the new inflatable arrives."

"Good idea. Could we plan to leave shortly after the New Year? Then we could restock all of the canned goods and other staples earlier than we planned for Ruth and Buddy's arrival."

"Yes, let's talk about it while playing sweep tomorrow."

"A million kisses to you, m'darlin'. Sofi will be thrilled. I don't know how May will react, but it will probably be easier on Sofi if we bring it up right in front of May anyway. She'll still have Raua, Andrea and Abu to help her out, so I think she'll be okay with the plan, don't you?

"Heaven only knows. I don't have a clue how May Fisher thinks."

Chapter 13

FIJIAN CHRISTMAS

Rog and I approached the Fisher Homestead about 10:00 the following morning. *"Ni sa yandra,"* I said proudly to Sofi as she opened the screen door, dressed in one of the teal-colored *Dreamer* T-shirts I had given her. The bottom of the T-shirt hung over a pink sarong printed with black and white fish. Her thick hair was casually swept up into a topknot, adding some height to her short stature.

"Good morning to you, too," she replied, equally proud of her English. We laughed as we gave each other a hug.

"Au damoni iko," I added and now Sofi really did look surprised although she knew it was true. "I love you,

too," she responded and we walked into the living room holding hands, followed by Rog, who could only shake his head at the two of us.

"*Ni sa yandra*," I repeated the greeting to May.

"Have a seat," she said, indicating the table they always used to play sweep. Andrea appeared with a deck of cards and Rog made himself comfortable in a worn stuffed chair, probably the only one in the entire village.

"Cut for deal," said May, who was Andrea's partner for the first round. Andrea won the deal and the first game of sweep began. To our delight, Sofi and I won that round and I wondered whether or not I should bring up the trip to Savusavu. I decided it wasn't the right time, since Andrea and Sofi were changing seats and May was already dealing out the cards. When May and Sofi won round two, I said, "Sofi, you must have learned all of Jack's tricks."

"I beat him anytime," she replied cockily, but we all knew it wasn't true. She was a good player, no doubt about it, but Jack was definitely better. When Andrea and Sofi disappeared after round two and returned with the promised scones, butter, jam and iced tea, I decided that this was my opportunity.

"May," I started, "Rog and I need some supplies from Savusavu. We'd be pleased to take Sofi and Loi with us shortly after the New Year so they can see Jack before he leaves for Australia. Raua, Andrea and Abu would still be here to help you out, so I'm asking your permission to take Sofi and Loi to Savusavu with us."

"When you planning to bring them back?" May asked.

"When Jack leaves for Australia."

"But nobody knows when that will be."

"That's true, but he told Sofi it would be by the end of January."

"And I take Debby and Loi to Raviravi Village on bus so Debby meet my Auntie," Sofi piped up.

"I think about it and tell you on Christmas Day," May said.

"Fair enough," I replied. "That's only ten days away. We can wait until then to know. By the way, these scones are delicious, as always. Who baked them this time?"

"Me," Sofi said with a laugh, "and with so much love. That's why they taste so good." I was glad to see she was happy, even though May had not said yes to the trip to Savusavu.

"May," I said, "your family is so large that it gets confusing for us *vavalangis* to keep everyone straight. If you start with you and Jack Fisher Senior and tell me the names of all your children and all of their children, I'll make a family tree from the information." I soon had all eight of her children's names written across the top of a page of paper entitled "May Covert and Jack Fisher." Under each name I wrote a "+" and under that, I wrote down the name of the spouse of each offspring. Under each spouse I listed their children as May rattled off the names. Most of them were common English names except for Sesel, Cika, Sia, Manoa, Fioni, Quenten, and

Sukuna, the young man who was killed by a shark the year before.

Abu came in fifteen minutes later. I learned that his real name was Albert and he was the twenty-six-year-old son of May's daughter, Margaret. When sweep resumed, Rog and Abu took on Sofi and Andrea, and May and I retired into the dining room where we used the large table to finish up most of the family tree. I was grateful to have all of this information, which helped me to keep everyone straight in my mind.

Abu came into the kitchen looking quite dejected. Rog followed him in. "Why Abu," I asked, "Did those crafty females beat you two?"

"No, it's something else."

"Uh-oh, what?"

"I don't know how to say this but . . ."

"But what?"

"Well, I've been over to Vodovodonabolo Bay several times in the *I Loi* since you've been gone. Sometimes I take Andrea with me, you know . . ."

"Yes?" I asked anxiously, thinking immediately of Glory.

"The first time we went over there after you left, Glory swam to the surface and came over to the boat."

"That's good," I said.

"Yes, but the second time we didn't see her, so the third time Andrea brought some bread and we threw chunks of it onto the water and still Glory did not come. Debby, I'm afraid she's gone. She's the most wonderful

128

fish I've ever encountered and I'm really sad, but something must have happened to her, or maybe she just left the bay. I don't know."

I had been so excited to see Sofi that I hadn't thought much about Glory until now. She was so special to me, so unusual, I didn't know what to say. I felt almost in shock. Finally I uttered, "Rog, I need to go back to Glory's Cove to see for myself if this is true."

"Honey, we can talk about it when we get back to the boat."

"Okay," I said numbly.

Everyone knew how sad I was and simply said, "*Moce mada*" or good-bye until later, as we headed for the door. I turned around to tell Abu that we needed to go to Taveuni with him two mornings hence.

"Yes, Sofi told me," he said. "I'll pick you up at 8:00."

"Okay, see you then," Rog said and we left as my eyes began to brim with tears.

The next day was a blur. I had experienced so many separations in life that I was shocked this one could affect me so deeply. I told myself that after all, Glory was only a fish. But then, that was the point. She was *not* just a fish. To me, Glory was a representative of God, sent with the message that God loved me, cherished me and heard my every prayer. Glory conveyed another message to me as well—that I should tell everyone how much they are loved and cherished by their Creator and that God hears their every cry.

I began to reprimand myself. Why had I left Glory's Cove when God was right there with me in the flesh, so to speak? I could have stopped in to see Glory on the way to Matagi or on the way back to Viani Bay after Matagi. Actually I wanted to, both times, but I was taking Roger's feelings into account. I knew from three years of sailing that he doesn't like making short stops in *Dreamer*. When Rog sets the hook in a cove or a bay, he likes to relax and stay for a while, and a while could be several weeks or several months.

Rog was not the person swimming with Glory. He knew how much I loved her, but he had already stayed in Vodovodonabolo Bay for two and a half weeks so that I could fully experience Glory and I had been back four times since to see her: first, when saying good-bye to Rik, Ann, Paul and Dianne; second, on Fiji Day; third, with Sofi to photograph Glory; and fourth, to fish-sit for her while the Fijians were net fishing.

"I guess that should have been enough," I reasoned, but another part of me argued back, *"But we're talking about God here!"*

I continued to rebuke myself throughout the day, whenever the thought hit my broken heart that I would never see Glory again. I would never watch her swim again; I would never marvel at her beauty again; I would never watch her chomping away on the hard coral again with her powerful jaws and teeth; I would never swim with her again; I would never communicate physically and telepathically with her again.

130

I busied myself making shopping lists for *Dreamer* and also for other Viani Bay residents to whom I wanted to give Christmas presents. I went through the treasures we already had on board: a pair of my gold earrings for Sofi; T-shirts and fishing lures for Jack and Abu; music tapes for Loi and some of her friends; a string of pearls for May; and planet Earth beach balls for Pamela, age four, and Sara, age five.

I still needed so much more. I jotted down names and next to each one, wrote what I already had on board for him or her or what I needed to buy. I passed the day this way, every once in a while sharing my grief over Glory with Rog. He was a good listener and didn't try to fix me. I was grateful for his understanding. When I mentioned again wanting to go back to Glory's Cove, he replied, "M'darlin', we have to go shopping tomorrow. On the 20th you are supposed to play Christmas carols for the children. Three days later is Sara Fisher's birthday party and you promised May you'd take photos. Two days after that is Christmas. After Christmas we can go back to Vodovodonabolo Bay and spend a week or two there."

"Okay," I agreed. "That will work."

The next day Abu picked us up with a full load of passengers already on board the *I Loi*. I was secretly relieved that neither Sofi nor Andrea was on board because I didn't want them to know anything about the Christmas presents I was planning to buy. When we reached Taveuni I headed straight to the variety store where I purchased some ribbon and Fijian wrapping paper with fish on it that almost made me cry again. I asked the clerk to cover the contents of my bags with some tissue paper so no one on the *I Loi* would suspect we were giving them gifts.

Then I hit the various food stores, purchasing what we needed until our planned trip to Savusavu where a more modern grocery store was located. Next, I walked to the bank, our prearranged meeting place, where Rog had just finished ordering the new inflatable. Abu was there and asked how I was doing, but immediately wished he hadn't when my eyes filled again with tears. "We are going to go back to Glory's Cove for a week or two after Christmas to see for ourselves," I told him. "Hopefully, Glory just got shy when she knew I wasn't on board the *I Loi* with you and Andrea."

"I hope you're right," he said gently.

There was no side trip to the Cannibal Café and I suddenly realized I was also missing Jack. Rog felt the same way, so we could only imagine how Sofi must be feeling. I figured that Christmas was going to be a bit difficult, even though we were all trying to be cheerful.

On Dec.19th, I practiced Christmas carols on the guitar, realizing that since I couldn't remember all the chords, I'd have to bring my music stand and three-ring-binder along with me the next day. But after breakfast the next morning, it was *so hot* I just didn't feel like going ashore with all of the stuff I needed to play carols for the kids. Besides, I was still blue and hurting over the possible loss of Glory.

"Don't go, then," Rog said.

"Yes, but I promised," I moaned, "and Sofi and Aseta will be waiting for me with the kids, and maybe even May. It's times like this when I wish we all had telephones."

"We don't, and I say just don't go if you're not up to it."

"*My dearly beloved spouse doesn't have a co-dependent bone in his body*," I thought to myself. I wished it were that easy for me to just not show up. I was dripping with sweat. Although it was only about 10:00 a.m., it was already ninety-five degrees with ninety-five percent humidity. Roger's face was all red and sweaty as well. "Maybe I should at least go ashore and tell them I'm not coming," I suggested.

"You know how well that will go over. They'll beg you to come back here and get your guitar. Worse yet, they'll all come back here with you."

"Oh Rog, I doubt that. But I think you're right. They'll talk me into coming back to get the guitar and I probably won't even be able to play it, the way my hands are sweating. My fingers will slip right off the strings."

"I said it once and I'll say it again, don't go. Stay here and relax. Don't you have a whole bunch of Christmas presents to wrap?"

One part of me thought he was right while the other part thought he was wrong. But two things were certain. I didn't want to go and he didn't want to talk about it anymore. So I started wrapping Christmas gifts and affixing little notes to each gift. This took the better part of the five remaining days before Christmas, but it was a labor of love I thoroughly enjoyed. I had such warm feelings towards each person as I wrapped his or her gift. When I finally finished, there were eighty presents ready for the villagers.

On the afternoon of December 23rd, we saw the *I Loi* approaching with none other than Jack Fisher at the helm! I couldn't believe my eyes.

"Jack," I hollered loudly, waving my arms and jumping up and down with excitement as he pulled alongside us. Still astounding me with his incredible dexterity, Jack nimbly came aboard.

"I can't believe you're here, but I'm so happy to see you, thrilled, in fact. Sofi must be over the moon that you're home. What's going on? Sit down and tell us everything."

It seemed that Jack's crewing job on *Galaxy* had just not worked out. He came home over the mountains in a friend's pick-up truck and arrived back in Viani Bay the night before to be here for Sara's twenty-first birthday celebration. Sara was one of Jack's favorite nieces; it would be important to her that he be there. Jack intended to stay for Christmas, then get a ride back to Savusavu where he now had a job on a fishing boat.

"Will you stay at the Homestead while you're here?" Rog asked.

"Yes, but only for these four days, then I'm gone."

"For good?" I asked.

"Probably. Sofi told me that you will bring her and Loi to Savusavu with you in early January. We're both grateful to you for that. I talked with Mom about it last night and I told her, 'Look, Sofi is no longer beholden to you and neither am I. We can live our lives where and when we want and I need to make money so that Loi can continue her education. I have a job in Savusavu. If Sofi wants to be there with me, she's twenty-eight years old and can do whatever she wants.'"

"Amen," I said.

"There's something else I have to tell you."

"Go ahead, Jack. Whatever you tell us will stay right here with us."

"I love my family dearly and I always will—all of them. I believe that what happened with my brothers and my mother taking away my inheritance was due to black magic. There are people who feel that I have wronged them in some way and they've put a black magic spell on me."

"Jack, do you honestly believe that?" I asked.

"You know, everybody has a past and everybody makes mistakes. I've made my share of them—now I'm reaping what I've sown."

"But surely you believe that God will protect you?"

"No, I don't. I believe the Bible is right when it says, 'What you reap is what you sow.' I can feel the black magic spells when they come at me and this is not the first time I've felt them. They frighten me because of the power of the senders."

"Jack, I can only say this," I replied. "I will pray for you and I will envision you surrounded by a protective white light."

"Thank you," he said, a bit choked up.

I loved this man very much and wrapped my arms around him. His understanding of the law of karma was different from mine, but the end result was still the same —you reap what you sow, sometimes in this lifetime and sometimes in a subsequent one. Nonetheless, that is cosmic law, just as the Bible said so succinctly.

"By the way," Jack said looking at me, "You could be in a bit of trouble yourself."

"How so?"

"Mom is angry with you for not showing up to sing Christmas carols for the kids last Saturday. They waited and waited for you until they finally gave up. And Sofi is mad at you for not coming ashore since your day at the Homestead playing sweep."

"Oh dear! I knew I was making a big social blunder, but Jack, it is *kata kata*, so very hot. You told us back in early October that it didn't get much hotter than it was then, but it must be at least ten degrees hotter now. It's really oppressive for us *vavalangis*, isn't it, Rog?"

"Yes, ma'am," Rog replied emphatically, the beads of sweat trickling down his reddened forehead and neck lending credence to his words.

"I've felt immobilized by the heat all week, which is also why I haven't spent any time with Sofi. It's times like these I really wish you had a VHF radio in Viani Bay. By the way, did you hear the sad news about Glory?"

"No. What happened?"

"Abu told me that she's not in her bay. I know that *cumudamus* don't live forever, but I just can't believe she's gone. We'll go after Christmas so I can see for myself whether she's there or not."

"We'll all be sad if Glory is gone," Jack said. "She's become a legend already in Viani Bay. No one has ever before seen a *cumudamu* befriend a human being. It's really quite amazing and we often talk about the two of you swimming and playing together."

"I'm convinced that God is orchestrating her actions to show all of us how very much He loves us and how special each one of us is to Him," I replied.

"I don't know whether I'd go that far," Jack said.

"Well, how else would you explain what's happening with Glory?"

"I don't know."

I looked at my watch and noticed that it was already 2:45 p.m. "Jack, what time does Sara's party start?" I asked.

"About now."

"Shouldn't we start heading in?" I grabbed the waterproof Pelican case containing our Canon EOS 10S, several lenses and two rolls of slide film. I headed forward to our stateroom to once again put on my Indian print wraparound skirt and the sleeveless gold-colored blouse.

When I returned, Rog and I boarded *Gos*, Pelican case in hand, and followed Jack to shore.

"Wow, there are gobs of people here," I said to Rog as we carried *Gos* above the high water line. "Now I'm probably in trouble for being late."

We followed closely behind Jack as if he could protect me from his mother's scorn, but as soon as I spotted May Fisher I headed straight for her. "May, I apologize for not showing up for the carol-sing on Saturday. Honestly, I was overwhelmed by the heat here at this time of the year."

She looked at me disapprovingly. "And now you late for Sara's birthday party and you keep Jack on your boat for hours so he late, too."

"I'm sorry."

I sensed my apologies were not accepted and my audience was over with her for the day. I got out the camera and busied myself shooting Sara, her friends and the extensive extended family. After reaching Savusavu, I'd have many rolls of film developed from our Viani Bay adventures. May and the family would be delighted when they received these prints, but in the meantime, I was in the doghouse. Even Sofi found partying with the villagers preferable to hanging out with me during Sara's party.

I wasn't sure whether it was Glory's influence or not, but my self-assurance and internal joy had increased tremendously since that day three and a half years earlier in French Polynesia, the day when tears trickled down my cheeks while I sat high above the surface of the water in our bosun's chair. While I knew that May and Sofi were upset with me, their disapproval rolled over my shoulders like gray clouds over an airplane's wings. I wasn't ruffled. Their judgmental attitudes were only hurting them, not me. I found the heat more troublesome than their scorn. Besides, I had a job to do. I enjoyed photography so it was fun for me to concentrate on obtaining high quality portraits, together with photos that reflected the beauty of the day and the joy of the participants. I also knew something that May and Sofi did not know. In two days, Rog and I would be showering them with love, not only with hugs and smiles, but also with the physical gifts we'd be giving them.

After I took the photos of Sara in traditional *tapa cloth* garb during her coming of age ceremony, she changed into modern Fijian clothing for the opening of her many gifts. This consumed the second roll of film, then Rog and I returned to *Dreamer*.

We made sure to be on time for the Christmas festivities. In fact, we arrived about thirty minutes early, with three large canvas carry-bags filled to overflowing with the gifts I had so carefully wrapped. While the women were cooking, I arranged all eighty of these presents on one of the buffet tables.

Before any gifts were opened, we all relished the Christmas feast, dining on succulent pork, chicken in curry and coconut cream, baked taro root, boiled spinach with onions, fried eggplant and sugar bananas. Then the children couldn't stand it any longer. They came up one by one as I handed a gift to each person. There were lots of ooh's, aah's and laughter as the villagers opened their gifts. I gave solid gold Gordian knot earrings to Sofi but within an hour, Loi had already lost one of them. I tried hard to stay detached, especially since a dear friend had given me those earrings as a farewell gift thirteen years earlier.

I gave Andrea the scarab bracelet I had treasured for many years. It was a fitting gift for this stunning young woman. The gift I was most excited about, though, was a bound, hard-cover journal full of blank pages for Sofi and Jack to use as a friendship book for the yachties to sign when they visited Viani Bay. I had already filled in the first two pages with photos of Rog, me and *Dreamer*, together with a heart-felt message. They were as thrilled as I'd hoped they would be.

They had written in our friendship book the year before, so they knew what a treasure these books can become, living documentaries of people who touch our lives in special ways. I also brought our friendship book ashore for Andrea and Abu to sign, asking that they return it to us before we would leave for Savusavu.

After all the gifts were opened, Jack's oldest brother, Sesel, stood up and made a speech thanking Rog and me for all the gifts. His exact words were, "No one has ever done this for us before." He added that the villagers had nothing to give to us in return, but in truth, they showed us their love and hospitality every day and brought us gifts of fruits, vegetables and fish from time to time. Besides, no material gifts could ever replace the many wonderful experiences we had had in Viani Bay, especially with Jack and Sofi. By the end of Christmas Day, I felt exonerated for not showing up at the Christmas carol sing-a-long and being a little bit late for Sara's birthday party. May even gave us permission to take Sofi and Loi to Savusavu.

Assuring Sofi we would return shortly after New Year's, we left Viani Bay two days after Christmas to look for Glory. Sofi placed two bags filled with mangos, bananas, pawpaws, green beans and eggplants into *Gos*. Then she handed me back my friendship book. I gave Sofi a big hug, whispering into her ear, "*Au damoni iko*. See you soon!"

Returning to *Dreamer*, I stowed the fresh produce, then eagerly opened the friendship book. In addition to their endearing personal message to Rog and me, I was stunned to find that the macho spear-fisherman Abu had composed the following "Ode to Glory":

> Oh Glory my friend, how awesome and pretty you are,
> Your friendliness will never fade from me.
> You are the sunshine and beauty of my life,
> Wherever I am, your name brings me pride.
>
> Chorus: So I'll sing your name, Glory my Glory,
> You are my life, you are in my heart.
> So I'll sing your name, Glory my Glory,
> How friendly you are, how great you are.

Famous is your name, please Glory come back to me.
My heart aches when you are not there.
I pretend that is nothing, but knowing you for so long
Makes it hard to believe that you are gone.

Repeat Chorus.

While I was deeply touched by Abu's poem, the last
verse saddened me immensely. Still, I was determined to
think positively. Although Glory was willing to share
herself with other human beings when I was around,
perhaps she was sent especially to me in answer to my
prayers. I wanted to think so.

Rog and I hoisted the anchor at 11:30 and powered
over to Vodovodonabolo Bay, a distance of some four
nautical miles, arriving an hour later. Rog was up at the
windlass letting out the anchor chain when I spied Glory
swimming near our stern! I was so excited, I almost let go
of the helm right then and there to jump into the water. I
was close to tears, my gratitude was so intense.

As soon as all the chain was let out, I ran below to
get a piece of bread to feed her. Next, I put on my mask,
snorkel and fins and swam with her. I held very still in the
water at first, letting her get used to me again. Then I
swam along after her for some time before she
disappeared into the depths. Again on *Dreamer*, I looked
back through our log. It had been exactly ten weeks since
the last time I'd seen her, the day I fish-sat while the
Fijians were net fishing. I could barely contain my
excitement all afternoon and evening. Glory was alive!!!

Chapter 14

A REAL BEAUTY

The next morning I awoke with a grateful heart and immediately went topside to see whether Glory was waiting for me. Bless her soul, she was already swimming around *Dreamer* and our numinous relationship filled my heart to the brim. I was torn between offering my thanksgiving to God formally in prayer and meditation or allowing my interactions with Glory to be my meditation. I chose the latter, tiptoeing slowly down the ladder in my bikini, mask and snorkel, but without fins.

When I saw her watching me descend the ladder, I sent her my love. What a gorgeous little creature she was, her thick blue and green diamond-shaped scales forming an iridescent suit of armor. Flanked by those dark lines that looked like eyeliner, her bulging green eyes seemed to be studying me intently, even as I was studying her.

Glory's small powder blue pectoral fins fluttered rapidly, her version of treading water. This stabilized her position so we could visit with each other. Her shape was an almost perfect oval, terminating at one end in her small mouth, accentuated with the divine coral color that first brought her to my attention. At the opposite end, the scales stopped and her caudal fin, or tail, began. Like her dorsal and anal fins, this caudal fin was bordered with bright yellow and an adjacent black stripe, and then a blue stripe followed by the blue-green color of the scales. The outlines of the small bones within all of the fins were clearly visible, like the veins of maple leaves in autumn.

I swam away from Glory as I had done on our very first swim together. She followed, then took the lead and guided me over to her little bommie. I watched her intently, noting in particular how she used her caudal fin. She kept it expanded to its full height when swimming in a straight line as it aided in the propulsion of her body through the water. However, whenever she turned, she contracted the height of this tail and used it as a rudder, moving it right or left depending upon which way she wanted to turn her body. Then she'd re-expand it to its full height and give a few swishes back and forth to swim in a forward direction.

The warmer summer water was filled now with plankton, making it somewhat difficult for me to see clearly at a distance. Nevertheless, the top of Glory's bommie was close enough to the surface for me to watch her dive down and then, in a headstand position, use her fanned out, expanded caudal fin to help her aggressively attack the hard coral. I had watched Glory do this time and time again. Despite her small mouth, her large sharp incisor-like teeth enabled her to hack away at the hard coral, which she actually ate.

Glory's teeth could also crack the exoskeletons of lobsters, clams and other crustaceans. She ate spiny sea urchins by blowing a strong jet of water at the urchin's base to lift it off the ocean floor. She would then roll the urchin over to expose its vulnerable underside.

In her headstand position, Glory also blew powerful jets of water onto a sandy spot between the coral heads to unearth prey such as sand dollars and starfish. She used her sharp teeth to grind a clam's shell into tiny pieces to remove the soft flesh. She even ate jellyfish! I felt fortunate that Glory had never exhibited aggressive behavior towards me, which triggerfish are known to do when threatened, especially if guarding their eggs. The bite of a giant triggerfish can remove a finger in seconds.

Besides her large sharp teeth and the coat of armor formed by her large bony scales, Glory had another defense mechanism—her first dorsal fin located just aft of her eyes. Normally, this fin is unseen because it lies flat against the top of the body. However, if alarmed, Glory could scoot into a crevice or hole in the reef and safely lodge herself in place by triggering her dorsal fin into an upright position. This fin contains three large sharp spines.

The first one is locked into position by the second spine, and the only way to collapse the trigger is to depress the third spine. A triggerfish wedged into a crevice is extremely difficult to dislodge. They can also produce loud warning sounds to deter would-be attackers, either by grinding their teeth or by vibrating their swim bladder with special muscles.

After Glory finished feeding on the top of her bommie, she dove deep down and I lost sight of her. I hung out on the surface for a few minutes, waiting to see if she would return to resume our swim. When she didn't, I swam back to *Dreamer*, noticing by the hands on the brass ship's clock that Glory and I had been together about twenty minutes.

The next day, Abu and Andrea entered the cove and came over to *Dreamer* in a small punt with a makeshift awning for protection from the harsh rays of the summer sun. I was just telling them that Glory was indeed alive, but I hadn't yet seen her that day—when there she was. Of course, we were all elated. I went below to get a large piece of bread; then I put on my mask, snorkel and fins while Andrea started to feed Glory.

Instead of feeding Glory piece by piece, Andrea put out about eight to ten chunks at once. I kept drifting near the bread that Glory wanted, but she wouldn't come close to me to get it. Perhaps she felt nervous with all three of us interacting, fearing that we were luring her on with the bread in order to trap her? After Andrea and Abu left, I got far away from the bread chunks to allow her to finish eating them. Then she did swim around me for a few minutes before disappearing.

On December 30th, Glory showed up at *Dreamer* three times. I fed her around 5:00 a.m. At 7:00 she was still around so I put on my mask and snorkel and we swam for twenty minutes. She took me over to the west side of the bay where lo and behold, I saw her mate again. Then they both disappeared into the depths.

Roger went to Taveuni with Abu so he could call the Minister of Finance regarding our prolonged stay in Fiji. His second task was to purchase lettuce, tomatoes, a cucumber, some garlic and a lemon for our salad dressing. I was running the engine to draw down the temperature in the refrigerator and recharge the batteries when I saw Glory again, swimming around the stern, attracted no doubt by the sound of our engine. I had the strongest desire to jump in and swim with her a second time, but I knew Rog would emphatically disapprove of my leaving the engine running unattended, so I fought the temptation and instead sat on the stern and communed with her.

On the very last morning of that year, I took my guitar ashore to play and sing some tunes for the dive masters from Rainbow Reef Divers and their clients. Later, to make New Year's Eve special for Rog and me, I thawed the best looking mahi-mahi fillets in our freezer. I made up a jar of my special salad dressing using soy sauce, minced garlic, safflower oil, freshly squeezed lemon juice and honey. In the early evening, I put together our tossed green salad, always a special treat on board *Dreamer,* and

Rog uncovered the circular Magma barbecue grill mounted on our stern railing. He waited until I was finished making the salad, which I placed into our trusty, stainless steel refrigerator, fashioned by hand in New Zealand. This gave us time to be together in the cockpit as Rog broiled the fillets to perfection. While still warmer than we liked, the temperature had cooled off enough for us to thoroughly enjoy our last dinner of 1995.

After relishing our meal in the cozy intimacy of our cockpit, we talked about all of the many things we had to be grateful for, starting with each other. Glory was also high on my list, as were *Dreamer* and God's presence and protection. I realized that my vision and experience of God was changing. I could now feel God's presence in everything, especially in Nature but also in the non-sentient objects surrounding me. Everything was becoming alive and filled with God's love! I shared this awareness with Rog, who I knew had his own conscious contact with God that served him well.

Then I asked Rog if he'd like to participate in a burning bowl ceremony. I got out a pad of paper, giving one sheet to Rog and one to myself. On my piece I listed such things as low self-esteem, fear, regrets and judgments. We did not read each other's lists but instead performed a short ceremony offering our negative tendencies to God, asking Spirit to remove them from our physical, mental, emotional and spiritual bodies.

To further demonstrate our intent, we rolled up each sheet of paper and very carefully burned them on the downwind side of *Dreamer*, allowing the barely discernable, gentle zephyrs of breeze to carry the black specks out over the water where they landed with a faint sizzle. We envisioned ourselves free of these impediments; then headed to our bunk for an intimate welcoming in of the New Year.

As I was exercising on the bow early the next morning, I spied Glory swimming around the boat. Feeding her had become both a communion and a ritual between us. I threw each little chunk of bread in a different location, marveling at her intelligence and the beautiful movements of her fins and body as she maneuvered for each morsel. She made a distinctive chomping sound as she grabbed each piece and I could actually see her teeth when she ate the pieces I dropped close to *Dreamer*.

After I fed her one full slice of bread, I said, "Well, that's all there is, Glory. No more left," and within thirty seconds, she was gone. It seemed she knew what I'd said. Sometimes I fed her two slices, so it clearly had nothing to do with the quantity. She was so smart! Glory even watched as I moved my arm to throw the bread and went after it before it had even landed, like a dog playing catch with its master. To me, this was truly incredible, even though I saw it with my own eyes.

The following day, it was overcast during the afternoon. Always cautious when it came to the weather, Rog tuned into Arnold's weather broadcast on our ham radio, reporting back to me that the winds were expected to increase to thirty knots out of the east. He wanted to move back into Viani Bay, just west of Yanuyanu Island where the island would offer us more protection from a strong easterly wind.

We left Glory's Cove early that evening. Even though the average lifespan of a yellowmargin giant triggerfish is ten years and I knew that the villagers of Viani Bay would do their best not to spear her or catch her in their nets, my heart still sank at the thought of leaving my beloved Glory after what had been such a short visit.

Chapter 15

STARGAZING

The wind might have been fierce that night, but nestled just offshore Yanuyanu Island, we slept like babies in a gently rocking cradle. The next morning, I delighted in the sight of a gorgeous rainbow over the Fisher Homestead, along with a pair of white terns entertaining me with their aerial acrobatics. I knew that Aseta Fisher lived onshore so after my exercises and daily meditation on the foredeck, I suggested to Rog that we go ashore to visit her.

An hour later, we were sitting around Aseta's dining room table as the tall Tongan woman shared her nagging regrets. "If only I'd known Ed was going to leave us so suddenly, I never would have criticized him so often. I picked on him about the smallest, most unimportant things." I was sad to hear that she was apparently still obsessed with these indiscretions, using almost the exact same words she'd spoken to us three months earlier, right after Ed passed away.

Again I tried to comfort and reassure her. "Aseta, you are only human like the rest of us. I feel certain that Ed understands and forgives you totally. Imagine how much he still loves you." She seemed doubtful and I hoped she would find a way to forgive herself for not being perfect.

Changing the subject, she turned to Rog exclaiming, "I'm so embarrassed about these dining room chairs, so old and wobbly. I'm hoping to fix them, but I don't have any screws. Look, six of the eight chairs are missing screws."

Rog examined each chair, making a mental note of what to buy to repair them. "We're leaving in a few days for Savusavu, but we'll be back in a couple of months. If there's a hardware store there, I'll buy some machine screws for you."

Bidding her adieu with the Fijian phrase, "*Moce mada*," we boarded *Gos*. I dropped Rog off at *Dreamer* before heading across the bay for the Fisher Homestead. Even though I was certain Andrea and Abu had already told Sofi that Glory was still alive, I wanted to tell her myself. Since it was difficult for me to haul *Gos* ashore by myself, I anchored in the shallow water then hurried up the beautiful green lawn to the familiar dark red wooden home with its white shutters and tiny front porch.

Ascending the porch steps, I cried out, "Sofi, Sofi!" When she came to the door, I exclaimed, "Glory is alive! She's still alive!" Andrea was close on Sofi's heels and although she already knew the good news, the three of us nonetheless danced around in a circle together. It felt wonderful to share my unbridled joy with these understanding Fijian friends.

Of course, we also relayed the news to May who was having trouble believing this anomaly. I looked forward to having my film developed in Savusavu so that May could see for herself the photos of my now famous pet fish.

I told Sofi we were almost ready to leave for Savusavu and if she wished, she and Loi could come aboard the following evening. I looked over at May, who graciously nodded her head in approval. "Andrea, could you and Abu drop them off in time for dinner tomorrow night? We're anchored near Aseta's house."

"Yes," she replied, eyes sparkling. Any outing with Abu seemed to enliven her.

"Thanks May and Andrea. See you tomorrow night, Sofi."

When Sofi and Loi came on board the following evening, Loi bounced around the boat, exuberantly expressing her joy about the upcoming adventure. As Rog fired up the barbecue to grill two big walu fillets, I prepared the fresh string beans and eggplants Sofi had brought. We relaxed in the cockpit, sharing stories of our adventures together thus far and looking ahead to our upcoming trip to Raviravi Village. Sofi's eyes lit up as she spoke about seeing her Auntie. At bedtime, Loi adopted Poochie and Roadie, my two stuffed dogs, wrapping her arms around them as she curled up on the starboard settee, leaving the longer portside settee for Sofi.

Bright and early the next morning, I awoke to find Loi already in *Gos*, throwing chunks of Roger's homemade bread into the water with the hopes of catching a fish. To my horror, I saw her lunge forward and with her bare hands, scoop a gorgeous flatfish into the boat. As the fish flailed around in the bottom of the dinghy, injuring itself and ultimately dying in its search for life-giving seawater, I had to turn away. I'm sure that Sofi read my feelings. She quickly took the dead fish, placed it onto the cutting board mounted on the starboard side of our stern pulpit and proceeded to fillet it.

I busied myself helping Rog stow the dinghy on the foredeck and after a quick breakfast, we weighed anchor on a perfectly clear, windless morning. Sofi, Loi and I all stood guard at the bow pulpit to watch for bommies.

"Look, there's a sea turtle!" Loi exclaimed.

"Wow, I'd love to swim with one of those," I said. Sofi laughed at my enthusiasm.

"That make me think." Sofi said, "Now we sing Abu's words about Glory to music of church song, and Loi and I teach you how to sing it."

"That's great," I responded. "How do you know the words?"

"Andrea save words on Abu's paper after she copy words in friendship book."

"I definitely want to learn it," I said and with that, Sofi and Loi began to sing.

"I'm impressed that you both memorized the entire song," I said as they finished.

"That is our present for you," Sofi said and she impulsively gave me a hug, eyes glistening with a mixture of pride and love.

"Hey, are you three watching up there?" Roger yelled from the stern.

"I am," Loi yelled back.

"Of course," I said as Sofi called out, "Bommie on left."

Rog corrected and I said, "Whew, that was close!" We focused on watching below the surface until we passed the Great White Wall off to starboard. Based on the chart and our prior trip to Fawn Harbour, we knew there were no dangerous reefs between our current position and where we intended to spend the night.

Sofi and Loi both wanted to sail but there was no wind, forcing us to power all the way to Fawn Harbour over glassy waters. During the trip, we went over and over "Ode To Glory" until I could sing it from memory myself.

We arrived at our overnight destination by early afternoon, but were disappointed at the murkiness of the water in this shallow bay, just outside the mangrove trees where we planned to hide *Dreamer* in the event of a cyclone. But murky or not, we went swimming and played in the water, dunking and splashing each other. We even managed to swim a little bit before climbing the ladder and rinsing off with some fresh water from our onboard sun shower. This consisted of a large plastic bag that held about three gallons of water, along with a hose and a valve. Held aloft by the halyard, it hung above our foredeck. We used it by sitting on one of *Gos's* pontoons, then opening the valve at the end of the hose.

We were soon to learn that little Miss Loi was also a card shark. After four rounds of Sweep and lots of laughter, Loi was the overall winner for the afternoon.

"What happened to your lucky streak, Sofi?" I asked.

"Loi cheat," she chided.

"I don't think so, Sofi," I teased. "You sound a lot like Roger when he accuses me of cheating at gin rummy."

I prepared a simple spaghetti dinner. We were out of salad fixings, so I sautéed some carrots, onions and garlic in olive oil before adding the spaghetti sauce and canned sliced mushrooms into the saucepan. I also fried the very fresh flatfish fillets in butter. Although it was a simple meal, Sofi complimented the food, saying, "*Na kana maleka na kakana*" meaning the food is delicious.

156

On the other hand, thirteen-year-old Loi wasn't mincing any words when she gave her analysis of powering all day. "It's pretty boring when you can't sail, huh?"

"Yes, Loi, but that's another reason, besides the heat and threat of cyclones, why most of the yachties leave Fiji between November and April," Rog explained. "The good sailing winds don't blow here during the summer."

That night, we watched a video I hoped would capture Sofi's interest: my all-time favorite Rodgers and Hammerstein musical, "The King and I". Luckily, I guessed right. Afterward, I led the two young women topside for another type of entertainment. Sofi, Loi and I lay on the main cabin top with me in the middle. The sky was alive with dancing stars. I pointed out the three constellations that were part of the ship Argo: Vela, which was Argo's sail; Puppis, which was the stern of the ship; and Carina, which was the Argo's keel. The girls were astounded.

Next, I pointed out the constellations that represent animals: Taurus, the bull; Lepus, the hare; Canis Major, the large dog; Canis Minor, the small dog; and finally, Monoceros, the unicorn. I told them these animals had best be careful, because one of my favorite northern constellations was also visible in the southern hemisphere on that night: Orion, the hunter.

Loi wondered, "Where is The Southern Cross?"

"Loi, the earth spins 'round on its axis all the time and the axis also tilts slowly throughout the year, making some stars visible at certain times and other stars visible at other times. Right now we can't see The Southern Cross, although usually you can see it in your hemisphere." Warming to my subject I elaborated, "If you lived at thirty-four degrees south latitude, like in New Zealand or the very southern portions of Australia or South Africa, you would always see The Southern Cross in the night sky because it's what astrologers call a South Pole constellation. That means the closer you live to the South Pole, the more frequently The Southern Cross is visible. Right here, we're at sixteen degrees south latitude, which is much closer to the equator than to the South Pole, so The Southern Cross is visible only part of each night, depending upon what time of the year it is. Do you understand, Loi?"

"Sort of. I see The Southern Cross lots of times when I look up into the sky at night."

"Well, now you have other constellations you can look for at night. Of all the ones we just identified, which do you like the best?"

"Orion," she answered.

"Why is that?"

"I like those three stars in a row, and that bright area underneath them."

"The three stars in a row are called Orion's belt, and the bright spot underneath is where new stars are forming from hydrogen and other gases that are swirling around. It is called the Orion Nebula, or M42, and it is the nearest star-forming region to our own star, the Sun. See that really bright star to the left of Orion?"

"Yes," Sofi replied. "Very bright."

"That is Sirius in the large dog constellation. It is the brightest star in our sky. It is almost twice as bright as Canopus, which is the second brightest star in the sky."

"This is so exciting," Loi said. "Can you tell us more?"

"Sweetheart, I think that's enough for tonight. I'll write down some of these names for you tomorrow, and if we're still on *Dreamer* tomorrow night, we can look up into the sky again and find them all."

"Can I sleep out here under the stars?" Loi asked. "Maybe I'll see The Southern Cross in the middle of the night."

"Yes, you can sleep outside and you'll be able to see The Southern Cross later tonight. It will rise there, in the east, and set in the west, just like the sun. Goodnight, Loi. Goodnight, Sofi." I gave them each a kiss.

"Thank you for all the stars," Loi said.

"Yes, thank God for all the stars. I only told you their names."

I went below, not surprised to find Rog fast asleep in our bunk, and in no time at all, I was sawing Zs too.

Chapter 16

UP AND OVER

The next morning dawned clear and windless, resulting in another full day of powering all the way to Savusavu. I was disappointed for Sofi and Loi, who'd been looking forward to a much more active passage. As we putt-putted along, I asked Loi, "Did you stay up all night?"

"No," she said sheepishly. "I fell right to sleep."

"Well, that's good. Why don't we go below and I'll draw the constellations for you with their names and the special bright stars in each one."

"That will be great," Loi said. Sofi came too, and when we were finished that project we practiced singing "Ode to Glory" again along with other songs we all knew.

I pulled out a chart of Vanua Levu Island. Sofi showed me exactly where Raviravi Village was located and the approximate route that we would take to get there. We decided to leave the following morning. Sofi said it would take at least a half day to get to where we were going, and asked how long I wanted to stay.

"You cannot come back on Sunday because no drivers work that day," she added.

"Let's talk about this over lunch," I said as I began extracting sandwich materials from the galley. Our two main standbys in the sandwich department were peanut butter and jelly and canned corned beef with mustard. That day was PB&J. After talking it over, we decided that I would make the return trip back over the mountains on Saturday, rather than Monday. That would give me three days for the entire trip.

"Sofi and Loi, since we've had no wind the entire time, would you like to hear a true story that happened a year and a half ago, involving lots of wind, danger and giant waves?" I asked.

"Yes, please, tell us this story," Sofi replied.

"Okay. It happened May of '94, in the Pacific Ocean between New Zealand, Tonga and Fiji. We had already sailed up from New Zealand to the island of Yanuca, just southwest of your capital city, Suva. We'd been in Fiji about two weeks when I took our dinghy over to visit friends on another sailboat named *Hasty*. As I chatted with our friends Tom and Lynn Hohmann, I noticed the sky was getting quite dark and the wind was blowing harder and harder.

"Soon Rog was on the radio hailing *Hasty*, telling me to get back to *Dreamer* as fast as I could. The wind continued to increase and by the time I got closer to our boat, I was actually surfing down swells of water in *Gos*. The wind had also changed direction, blowing *Dreamer* toward a lee shore. Rog had started the engine to keep pressure off the anchor, so we wouldn't be swept all the way ashore. It wasn't easy, but with Roger's help I managed to get back onto *Dreamer* and tie up *Gos*. The boat was pitching up and down and poor Rog had the difficult job of getting the anchor up while I continued powering *Dreamer* forward."

"Wow, what happened when the anchor was up?" Loi asked.

"I increased the speed of our engine, which you can probably tell is not very fast, so it was pretty scary, but the engine was strong enough to push through the wind and the waves to get us away from the shore."

"Where did you go?" Sofi asked.

"When Rog returned to the cockpit, I went forward in the blinding rain to try to see whether or not there were any reefs in front of us. Truly, it was an impossible job, and all I could do was pray that we didn't hit anything! In the meantime, *Hasty* had found safety on the other side of the island and radioed to guide us to them. When we finally anchored securely, Tom and Lynn invited us to come over, dry out, and have some of Lynn's homemade soup, which we happily accepted.

"While aboard *Hasty*, some other friends radioed to see whether we were all right. Sandy and Rondi of the yacht *Sundowner* told us a huge low pressure system was bumping into a huge high pressure system off of New Zealand, and that the fleet of ships sailing in the New Zealand Island Cruising Association's Tonga Regatta was now in big trouble."

"What is a low and high pressure system?" Loi asked.

"You ask the hardest questions sometimes, Loi. Well, let's see." I tried to explain. "It has to do with atmospheric pressure, measured by a barometer. Air pressure is the weight of all the tiny molecules of air above you."

"How come I don't get squashed then?"

"You have air inside your body too, and that air balances the pressure outside of you, so you stay nice and firm and don't get squashed. Isn't the way God figured all this out amazing!!

"Anyway," I continued, "air will rush from an area of high air pressure to an area of low pressure creating what we call wind. When the high pressure system is very high and the low pressure system is very low, the wind rushes very fast from the high system to the low system causing very high winds."

"I get it! That's really interesting."

"Rog, do you want to take over the story? You remember the names of all the sailing yachts and the rescue vessels."

Rog picked up where I left off. "As I remember, we stayed anchored for the next four days, listening to the radio channel that was being used by the New Zealand Marine Rescue Centre in Wellington. Our prayers went out to all the cruisers caught in this huge storm. We listened intently to the conversations between the rescue center and the Orion aircraft sent from New Zealand to assist the floundering fleet of thirty-five tiny sailboats, struggling to survive. According to the anemometer on the *Monowai*, one of the primary rescue vessels, the wind was blowing a steady sixty to sixty-five knots with gusts sometimes well over eighty knots, and waves were reported from sixteen to thirty-two feet high!

"Crews of three yachts, the *Mary T, Sofia* and *Destiny*, were personal friends of ours and we kept our prayers going for them constantly. Luckily, they all lived to tell many terrifying stories at the Royal Suva Yacht Club several weeks later.

"Although officially called The 1994 Queen's Birthday Storm, it was also nicknamed The Bomb, an unexpected, out-of-season cyclone that appeared out of nowhere and could not be detected by any weather faxes until it was too late. The fleet was caught half way between New Zealand and Tonga, right in the middle of this monstrous weather system that spanned a nine hundred mile radius.

"In total, five huge commercial and naval vessels headed into dangerous waters for some pretty hazardous rescue operations that removed twenty people from seven different yachts. Her Majesty's New Zealand research and survey ship, *Monowai,* performed three of the rescues. The Fijian cargo ship, *Tui Cakau III*; the New Zealand 340 ton fishing vessel, *San Te Maru 18*; the French warship, *Jacques Cartier*; and the Norwegian Bulk carrier, *Nomadic Dutchess* made up the rest of the rescue fleet. The seven sailing yachts were abandoned, left to fend for themselves.

"Sadly, the *Quartermaster* out of New Zealand sank with all three crew on board. The only remaining trace of them was their EPIRB, emergency position-indicating radio beacon, which continued relaying its signals to Wellington, New Zealand, long after *Quartermaster* had sunk. Not surprisingly, several crews gave up their voyages after their terrifying experience."

"We are happy that the *Dreamer* not get in storm," Sofi remarked as Rog finished his tale.

Loi agreed, asking the universal question of kids everywhere, "Are we almost there?"

"Yep, we're just turning into the outer harbor of Savusavu now," Rog answered, steering *Dreamer* around the buoys marking the reefs outside of the harbor. When we entered the inner harbor some fifteen minutes later, we could see the commercial buildings lining the waterfront. It sure looked different from Viani Bay, but it was still a tiny metropolis compared to the Fijian capital, Suva. Rog piloted *Dreamer* to the new floating gas dock that

166

connected to the shore by a ramp and before I finished tying our dock lines to the float, Sofi and Loi were ready to disembark with their few belongings.

"Hey, where are you two going?" I asked.

"To see friends," Sofi replied. Do not worry, Debby, but be ready to meet us tomorrow morning by 8:30."

"Where are we meeting?" I asked.

"See yellow buses?" She pointed to a place where six yellow school buses were parked. "You must look for bus to Natua."

"I thought we were going to Raviravi Village?"

"The bus not go that far. I make plan for us."

"How can you do that with no telephone?" I wondered.

"*Sega na leqa*," Sofi said, dismissing my worries.

"Are you sure you two will be all right? Do you want to stay on *Dreamer* until tomorrow morning? Are you going to see Jack?"

"No, Debby, it's okay. We be fine. Just be sure you at yellow bus to Natua on time."

"I'll be there. *Lako i sili*," I joked. "*Qai raice iko tale*," meaning go and take your bath. See you later.

By the time Sofi and Loi made their way over the ramp, Rog had finished fueling up and was now working on refilling our water tanks. I changed into my sundress and grabbed four large red and white canvas tote bags and two burgundy insulated bags, standard tools for our island shopping trips. Minor miracles always seemed to occur on these hunting and gathering expeditions. I'd go from one tiny store to another until I was able to purchase almost all of the items on my shopping list.

Somehow, everything would just fit into our fridge, canned storage bin, bilges, and the hanging nets for fruits, vegetables and pasta. And somehow there were no items that didn't find a home, yet no storage space remained unused. This happened time and time again and never ceased to amaze me.

In this port, there was one large, fairly modern grocery store named Morris Hedstrom. Before storing the goods we purchased there, we pulled away from the floating gas dock and chose our anchorage, directly offshore from the Copra Shed Marina. No Glory came up to the surface to greet us, and I found myself missing my faithful friend. Luckily, I didn't have much time to think about her. After dinner I packed one of our small, collapsible nylon suitcases for the trip; then Rog and I launched *Gos* so I could get to shore on time.

At 6:00 the next morning, I climbed over Rog and went out onto the foredeck in my skimpy muscle shirt for my exercises and meditation. I was a little self-conscious because other boats were anchored in the harbor, but I reminded myself that while I might be the center of my universe, I was not the center of anyone else's. I was appreciative to have time to center myself in the Divine Presence before setting forth on yet another Fijian adventure. I found myself greatly looking forward to experiencing Sofi's and Loi's unbridled joy at returning home.

When we reached the parked buses, none of them displayed any destinations above the front windows. It was already 8:25. Just then, I heard Sofi calling my name and looked around till we spotted her small, thin body leaning way out a bus window.

"Good luck, Honey," Rog said as I mounted the steps of the old, overcrowded bus to the loud squawking of many chickens. I squeezed my way back to the next to last seat where the three of us barely fit on the tattered cushion. Behind us was a long, single seat piled high with *yaqona* roots.

These roots were pulverized by hand and mixed with water, creating a substance called *kava*, a mildly narcotic Fijian grog that looked and tasted like mud. *Kava* was served from a large communal bowl, called a *tanoa*. Each person could request a "low tide," "half tide" or "high tide" serving from the host, who ladled the appropriate portion into a *bilo*, a coconut shell bowl. Then everyone clapped their hands three times, meaning "bottoms up," and the drinker was expected to down his serving in one fell swoop, like a shot.

In the old days, this *kava* ceremony was reserved for official visitations between village chiefs but as the years passed and standards relaxed, all the village men began participating. Eventually the ritual became a daily practice, much like drinking alcohol is in Western society, and more and more women began participating too. In some places, *kava* use has become quite a problem.

Whenever yachties arrive in a village, they are escorted to the village chief and expected to present *yaqona* roots they've purchased in Suva as a show of respect. The yachties then petition the chief for permission to anchor in the local bay or cove. If the chief says yes, then he becomes responsible for the yachties' safety during the period of time that they remain in his territory. I've never heard of a Fijian chief saying no.

Typically, the chief will ask what activities the yachties are planning and assign one or more villagers to accompany them, to show them local points of interest and provide for their safety and comfort. After this is sorted out, the community *kava* bowl comes out and people sit 'round the *tanoa*, drinking this intoxicating local beverage.

This is just one of the reasons why visiting Fiji by yacht is such a special experience—we met so many wonderful Fijians who truly took an interest in us. Some of the bonds we formed have lasted all these years since. As I looked at the pile of *yaqona* roots on the back seat of the bus, I suspected there would be a grog party for us in Raviravi Village.

As we pulled away, Rog took a photo of Sofi and me waving from the air conditioned bus. It was air conditioned because there literally was no glass in any of the windows. We headed around the harbor, the bus chugging along pretty well with its heavy load. The chickens squawked constantly as diesel exhaust poured in the rear window, but it was all part of the trip. My heart sang with gratitude at the opportunity to experience this local color first-hand.

The terrain changed as we headed up the mountain that formed the spine of Vanua Levu Island. We were traveling almost directly north and slightly west through the very center of the island, the vegetation just as lush as on the other eastern Fijian Islands we'd visited. If Fijian homes were scattered along our route, they were well hidden by the broad leaves of the tropical trees and plants.

As we continued our upward climb, our speed kept decreasing to the point where a fast jogger could have kept up with us. I asked Sofi whether we would all have to get out eventually and push and she laughed heartily. I joined in her laughter and sat back, enjoying being a passenger with no responsibilities.

We finally reached the summit to find overcast conditions on the north side of the island. The old school bus picked up speed like a runaway train and within fifteen minutes, we were in the small mountain town of Natua. Everyone began exiting the bus; women carried roosters, chickens and baked goods while young boys pushed their way to the back seat to retrieve their bundles of *yaqona* roots.

We were the last off the bus. With a twinkle in her eyes and an impish tilt to her head, Sofi instructed me to stay where I was as she and Loi scampered off, leaving me with my nylon overnight bag and my camera. Standing under gray skies, I looked around with interest. The small mountain town consisted mainly of one street, angled at about forty-five degrees with the slope of the mountain. In stark contrast to the overcast sky were the colorful saris of three young Indian women, who kindly allowed me to take their photo with the push here dummy or PhD camera I used when traveling light.

Indians had become well integrated into the culture of Fiji. In 1874, the islands were being torn apart by wars between the different chiefs and by cannibalism. Several chiefs invited the British in to help stabilize their country. The Englishmen who accepted this invitation wanted a profitable cash crop to seal the deal. Between 1879 and 1916, they transported hundreds of Indians from the overcrowded conditions in India to the gorgeous, lightly populated islands of Fiji, to cultivate and harvest sugar cane.

The Indians proved themselves hard workers, eventually establishing many successful businesses throughout the islands. The laid back Fijians, in contrast, continued with their agrarian lifestyles in the villages. The Fijians learned Hindi and also English, becoming a tri-lingual society.

However, problems arose as a result of restrictions in the Fijian constitution, which only allowed indigenous Fijians to own land. Exceptions were made in order for the English to have their sugar cane plantations. Some chiefs made other exceptions as well, such as when Jack

Fisher's grandfather built ships in exchange for land in the southeastern portion of Vanua Levu Island. But these exceptions were only granted to the English, never the Indian population.

The Fijian constitution also limits the number of non-indigenous Fijians who may hold government positions. As the Indians proved their capabilities in the business world, establishing successful stores and services throughout the country, they found themselves in a frustrating position—unable to own land or have any say in their government, creating a situation that's led to recurring tension between the two races over the years.

I was stirred from this reverie when two small hands covered my eyes from behind and a familiar giggle sounded in my ears.

"Why you little rascals! Where have you been?"

"Turn around," Sofi said. "See Loi in back of small truck?" I nodded at what looked like a small, grey-green army transport vehicle. Its canvas top just covered the low truck bed where Loi rested against a large burlap sack of rice. There were several other sacks in the truck bed, leaving just enough room between them and the spare tire for Sofi and me.

As I climbed in, I began to hear the telltale sounds of a downpour on the canvas top. Sofi's hair was already wet as she bounded in behind me, squishing into the only available spot left. I was thankful I'd brought very few belongings as I held the small nylon suitcase between my knees and chest.

Sofi whistled so the driver knew we were all securely inside, and off we went, charging down the mountainside towards the sea. Exhaust fumes wafted around us as we tried to talk, but it was too noisy. We were grateful for the canvas roof, but it wasn't long before I started feeling dampness through my cotton skirt.

"Uh, Sofi, do you feel what I feel?"

"No, what?"

"Loi, do you feel what I feel?"

"I think so," she replied. Loi sat near the right rear wheel and I near the left. The spinning tires hurled a stream of wet muddy water and gravel off the unpaved road and right onto our derrieres. I didn't know how the rice sacks were faring, but I knew I was going to be quite a sight by the time we reached Raviravi Village. At least it was hot out. Surrendering to the wet ride, I watched out the open back of the truck as the miles rolled by, and leaning back against a burlap sack, I fell asleep to the rhythm of the bouncy truck bed.

About an hour later, Sofi woke me up. "We go down Raviravi Hill right now. We be home in minutes." She and Loi were clearly excited. Sure enough, in about five minutes the vehicle came to a stop and before we could scramble out there were eleven unfamiliar faces gazing in at us.

"Sofi, Loi," they shouted. "What a grand surprise!" A pair of arms reached in to help Sofi out. Next out was Loi and then I managed to mobilize my constricted, damp limbs to climb out as well. I was introduced as Sofi's yachtie friend who had a pet fish named Glory. Of course, their curiosity was piqued. So it wasn't long before I found myself giving an abbreviated version of the unlikely relationship I'd enjoyed for the past four months with a *cumudamu*. Sofi insisted on singing "Ode to Glory" so we sang it with emotion, afterward announcing the good news that Glory was still alive and last swam with me on December 29th.

We walked across an open green to Auntie's house. As far as I could tell, at least six people lived in the large one-room dwelling with a wooden floor. An elderly woman with a head full of thick, white, unruly hair caught my attention right away. The distinct energy of matronly peace, harmony and love surrounded her despite her somewhat deformed body.

Sofi bent down and gave this woman a long hug, then introduced me to her Auntie, the woman who had raised her like her own child. Auntie's atrophied legs looked totally useless as they sprawled out on the floor in a bizarre configuration. I would have to encourage Sofi to warn me about such surprises in the future, but this was not the time since villagers were already arriving in a steady stream to welcome Sofi and Loi back home.

"I stay because Jack out fishing for two weeks, but Debby must go back Saturday, so we must show everything for her," Sofi told her friends.

"First, though, I'd like to change clothes and rinse my muddy skirt," I pleaded.

The rain had stopped before we reached the village, although the sky remained overcast. Sofi got me a towel and we walked maybe twenty yards towards the sea, where stood two shower stalls. Sofi handed me a bar of soap saying with a grin, "*Lako i sili.*"

"You too," I said, but she laughed and skipped away. When I came out of the shower stall there were a dozen children waiting. Before I knew it we were in a volleyball game, after which we all started to dance spontaneously from a natural joy. Suddenly I noticed everyone was looking at me, clapping rhythmically like the beat of a drum. "Keep dancing, Debby," they cried. Then some of the girls started to copy my flower child, 60's style dance moves.

With the encouragement of my admirers, I let it all hang out, doing my version of the bump and grind, the monkey, the Bristol stomp—whatever met my fancy— even the shimmy. Soon we were all dancing uninhibitedly. I couldn't even imagine this scene happening in Viani Bay where the English had had more influence over the years. No wonder Sofi was so excited about coming home!

Raviravi Village was situated on a high bluff overlooking the sea, but the houses were set back quite a distance from the bluff. I asked Sofi and the villagers to walk me down to see the water's edge, and while walking, I asked Sofi about her Auntie's paralysis.

"You know many Fiji women do net fishing for villages?" she began.

"Yes," I said. "I've seen this in several places in Fiji."

"Well, Auntie net fish for hours and hours with other women. Only here, water much colder than Viani Bay. Women always wear sarongs in water. When they bring fish home, they stand in front of wooden board over there and fillet fish with wet sarongs still on bodies. Wind blow hard here especially during winter and make Auntie's legs get very cold from wind and damp cloth, but she never complain. She tell me this after legs die.

"Now no can move legs from waist down, so you see Junior put hole in wooden floor. Underneath hole, there is bucket so Auntie can walk with hands over to hole for to go potty. No one looks. Someone cover hole when she finish and some people empty bucket every day."

"Did this happen to any of the other women?" I asked.

"Not in Raviravi Village," she replied. "I never hear or see this again."

"Wow, that is very sad," I said. "I will keep your Auntie in my prayers."

"Thank you," Sofi replied. We looked out over the open water. There was no land in sight as far as the eye could see. The water was calm now, but I could imagine it beating upon the beach below the bluff during the windy winter season.

"Would a yacht be safe anchored offshore here?" I asked.

"I not sure," Sofi responded. "During winter, water have many white caps and not friendly like Viani Bay and Somosomo Strait. I do not think you want to bring your *Dreamer* here. Better to stay in Viani Bay and come here by bus with me." She laughed as only Sofi can, giving me a hug.

"See punt on beach?" Sofi continued. "Those men near the boat dive for sea slugs. They bring bags up to village and spread out sea slugs to dry. We also say sea cucumbers."

"Oh." They didn't sound too appetizing to me.

The children's energy spiked again. One tagged me and said, "You're it!" and everyone ran. I easily tagged one of the girls and then ran off with Sofi to where the adults gathered for their evening volleyball game. They certainly outplayed me, so I chose to sit down and simply watch the second game. Seeing their enthusiasm, I could see how Loi became so good at this game. Even Sofi was a decent player, but a few more inches of height would have really helped her.

Finally we went back to the house to unpack our things. In addition to Sofi's cousins, there was a pretty young girl in the room near the beds who looked a little bit like Loi. Sofi introduced me, "Debby, this is my daughter, Luciana Divamaiwai."

"It is so good to meet you, Luciana," I said, staring into her beautiful brown eyes. Her demeanor was much calmer than Loi's almost perpetual motion. She gave her mother a hug, then walked over to the kitchen area to help with the meal preparations.

"Sofi, you are full of surprises," I exclaimed. "I can't believe you never told me you had another daughter, you rascal, you. She is beautiful. Why did you leave her behind?"

"She one year younger than Loi and have many friends here in Raviravi Village. She love daddy more than Loi do, so Auntie tell me leave her here. The village take care of her. My Loi and Jack and May keep me very busy so I not miss Luciana too much. I know she be okay."

I was speechless. While I have read that Native American children are still raised by communities, extended families living in one home or even in the same community is basically a thing of the past in modern day America.

No one would let me help with the food preparation. Instead, some of us played sweep while the others worked with the food. More folks piled into the house, giving Sofi and Loi welcoming hugs, until we had about two dozen people for a wonderful dinner of curried chicken, cassava, Fijian spinach and custard for dessert. About an hour after dinner, everyone but Auntie left for a *meke* at the community hall. In this traditional Fijian dance, the all-female dancers dress in special costumes and tell a story with their hands, moving only their upper bodies from a seated position on the ground.

After the *meke*, I wasn't surprised to hear the sounds of clapping for "bottoms up" coming from a group of men gathered around a community *kava* bowl. One of Sofi's female friends invited us over to the *tanoa* as well. We had a couple of half tide *bilos* and by the time we heard the sound of bongos and guitars, I was ready to dance. Junior and I began dancing but to my surprise, only six other people joined us. The others sat around the *kava* bowl or leaned against the wall in a *kava*-induced, semi-comatose state. I was pleased to see that they weren't so stoned that they couldn't clap and cheer on the dancers and musicians. I kept dancing until finally I tired and asked Sofi to walk me back to the house. It had been a long day.

Sofi secured the mosquito netting around my bed, saying that she was going back to the party and would come to bed later. Loi and her sister were already fast asleep on the other bed. Auntie and her family would all sleep on the floor so that we could have the beds. I tossed and turned for a while, but finally drifted off, dreaming of Fijians dancing joyously in the hall.

The next morning, I felt too self-conscious to get up and do my exercises and meditation, so I lay quietly in the comfortable bed and meditated until the household began to stir. I was in for another delightful day of activities, starting with a breakfast of scones and milk.

Many children gathered at the house and I soon found myself playing tag with them on the village green. They begged me to dance for them again but I told them they had to dance along with me. Just when I was beginning to wear out, Sofi said it was time to go visit her best childhood friend, Alani Seniceva.

Alani's youngest child was Loi's age so the two youngsters ran off to have their own fun. Then the two women took me through the neighborhood to meet more of Sofi's friends. A young woman named Fanny had an adorable four-month-old baby girl named Melaia Raravitu. Fanny proudly informed me she'd spoken to her husband the night before and they had decided to insert the name Debby between Melaia and Raravitu so the baby would become a great dancer. I told her I felt honored, to say the least.

We went back to Alani's house for a light lunch. The village was having a church fundraiser that night and Alani invited me to wear one of her sarongs for the event. I picked a bright red one. Then, carrying the borrowed sarong, we went to see the sea slugs drying. I thought they looked grotesque: long, black worms about eighteen inches in length and six inches around that were just beginning to shrink from dehydration. I was relieved no one had yet asked me to eat one. Alani explained that the Fijians did not eat them either, but exported them to Japan, where they were considered a delicacy.

After another round of tag with the ever-present children, we returned to Auntie's home for a couple of hours of sweep. Before dinner, everyone wanted to hear about Glory, so I told the gathering all about our various swims together and how Glory had graced the Fijians of Viani Bay with her presence when they came to

Vodovodonabolo Bay for Fiji Day. Sofi took over the story, telling everyone that Abu, the avid spear fisherman, was so enthralled by Glory that he had written "Ode to Glory," which Sofi and I then sang for them. Like May, Auntie looked totally baffled.

Sofi convinced me that we had a long night ahead of us and I should take a nap. After dinner, I changed into Alani's sarong. Then we went back to the community hall for the church fundraiser, where villagers bought each other's baked goods, woven baskets and trays, jewelry and second hand clothing. When the sale was deemed over, we all went over to the church for a short sermon. The collection basket was passed around and the most beautiful portion of the service began, the a cappella singing. With ardent fervor, hymns of praise rang out in multiple layers of exquisite harmony that uplifted my soul to lofty heights. To me, this was a glorious way to end a wonderful visit.

Early the next morning, a troupe of ten set forth. Only three of us were traveling; the others came along to see us off. First we walked about a mile and a half along a rutty, muddy road to get to Jack-the-Indian's house. We picked delicious mangoes in his yard, then helped him to push his pick-up truck down his long muddy driveway; otherwise it would keep getting stuck. At the end of the driveway, the two other travelers and I piled in and I bid Sofi and Loi good-bye. We rode about six miles in the pick-up truck to the home of another Indian man who drove the local bus. He took us through the beautiful countryside back to Natua, where I disembarked to catch the bus back up and over the mountain to Savusavu. It was a gorgeous, thoroughly uneventful trip.

I got back to Savusavu on Saturday afternoon and Rog took me out to lunch. I babbled for two whole hours, telling him all of the little nuances and adventures of my visit. On Monday morning, I felt a little tired and a bit dizzy when I got up. By the afternoon, my temperature reached 102.2 degrees Fahrenheit. I guess Spirit was indeed watching over me when I arranged to come home on Saturday instead of Monday.

Chapter 17

TWO MONTHS IN SAVUSAVU

After I recuperated, Rog and I took a few trips ashore to take advantage of the services offered in Savusavu. One of the first things I did was send off my fifteen rolls of thirty-six-exposure slide film to be processed in Suva. Rog picked up machine screws, washers and nuts for Aseta, enough so she'd have extras in case of further dining room chair breakdowns. I ordered a lightweight sundress from a local seamstress who offered a lovely selection of thin cotton, tie-dyed fabrics. From the leftovers, she also made a broad headband to tie back my long, curly hair and keep it off my neck.

Every once in a while someone would drop off either Jack or Sofi at *Dreamer,* but not both at the same time. During their separate visits, we heard the continuing saga of their trials and tribulations in Savusavu, where Jack was working for almost no pay on a Fijian fishing boat. Sofi was angry and irritable, accusing Jack of drinking too much and not giving her any money to support Loi's education. According to Jack, Sofi spent her time at grog parties while he was out on the fishing boat for a week or more at a time.

Basically, we tried to be good listeners, stay out of the middle, and keep them both in our prayers. We hoped the distractions of the big city would not tear them apart. Having lived through addiction ourselves, we knew a little of what they were going through, and could only encourage them each to be accountable for their own behavior and try to criticize each other less.

We restocked our food supply, oil filters, rebel lures for fishing and other cruising necessities. We also bought a fifteen horsepower Mercury outboard for our new dinghy from Curly Carswell, the Kiwi-born proprietor of both Sea (Fiji) Ltd. and Eco Divers. The lean, perpetually suntanned Curly had lived in Fiji for twenty-three years and posed a striking image with his long white hair and almost equally long white beard, reminding me of a slender Santa. Curly spearheaded the campaign to acquire the South Pacific's first ever decompression chamber, auctioning off his famed beard to the highest bidder in 1993 for eleven hundred dollars.

We moved *Dreamer* to outer Savusavu Bay. Although only five miles away, the water was clear again and this change of scenery relieved some of the claustrophobia I felt while anchored in the inner harbor. We were anchored a quarter of a mile offshore from the beautiful Jean-Michel Cousteau Resort with its manicured, rolling green lawns, stately palms and gorgeous bures with their lovely thatched roofs.

Two miles of underwater reef lay just south of the resort at the entrance to the outer bay. Closer to *Dreamer* was a beautiful coral head named Split Rock that I visited frequently, wearing my mask, snorkel and fins. It was home to a profusion of fish and soft corals and reminded me of my many excursions with Glory.

Rog and I went ashore to the resort one afternoon to tour the premises and watch an outstanding slide show of underwater photos, complete with commentary. One of the staff divers gave me some hints regarding underwater photography which I put to good use during the upcoming dives we'd arranged with Eco Divers.

We talked with Jean-Michel about his famous father, Jacque, and also about the 1985 incident that resulted in the destruction of the Green Peace vessel, *Rainbow Warrior*. The ship was destroyed by the French while protesting that government's nuclear testing in the Tuamotus Atolls of French Polynesia. Despite the unflattering light in which this event portrayed his country, Jean-Michel remained gracious, supporting our viewpoint on the conservation of marine life in these otherwise untainted waters.

Two other cruising families we knew were anchored near us: James, Anita and Sparky Merriman on *Starlight* and Joe, Katie and Kyle Crisp on *Mundaca*. The two energetic sons, Sparky and Kyle, were seven and five years old, respectively. I was impressed by just how much these parents did for their children. Along with the normal care and discipline, these cruising parents also had to be their kids' schoolteachers, doctors and nurses.

During our time in outer Savusavu Bay, seven-year-old Sparky developed a fever which soared to 104.1 degrees Fahrenheit. Medical books were piled high in their cabin as Anita asked anxiously, "Does your neck feel stiff? Is there any pain in your knees when you bend your legs?"

"No," the little boy replied. His parents were beside themselves trying to figure out what was wrong, but finally, after the administration of several ice baths, Sparky himself suggested, "Hey Dad, why don't you shine the flashlight in my mouth?" Lo and behold, his tonsils were swollen and red with white dots on top. James and Anita were so relieved to identify the fever as tonsillitis, and quickly gave Sparky the appropriate antibiotic.

Most cruising families stock up on emergency medications before leaving their home ports, with the help of reference books and their doctors' recommendations. Rog and I had purchased six hundred dollars' worth of such supplies before leaving California, storing it all in Tupperware containers stowed in the coolest, darkest locations we could find on board.

Jack was still able to visit us occasionally, even in the outer bay. During one of his visits, we sat in our cockpit enjoying the shade provided by our canvas dodger and talking about diving. When the subject got around to shark attacks, Rog said, "When Deb and I took our scuba diving classes, the instructor told us sharks don't like the taste of human flesh. Their vision is not good and when they attack a surfer, they think the combination of the surfer and the board is a seal, which they dearly love to eat. One bite out of the surfer, though, and they know they got the wrong morsel!"

"I agree," Jack responded. "You remember when my nephew Sukuna was attacked and killed off the northern tip of Taveuni Island? You were in Viani Bay, right?"

"Yep, we attended the funeral and Deb took photos for your brother Chris and his family."

"Well," Jack went on. "I'm convinced that shark would never have attacked Sukuna if he hadn't been diving with a speared fish dangling from his waist. It was the fish the shark was after, not Sukuna. Otherwise he would have polished off my nephew and there would not have been a body to photograph at the funeral. Sukuna had three dive buddies with him on that trip and I talked with one of them for a long time at the funeral. He gave me all the gruesome details."

"I don't know whether I want to hear this, Jack, but go ahead," I said.

"These four young men worked in pairs. They anchored their punt just off the northern tip of Taveuni, not far offshore. The two diving each wore a long line around their waists with a float attached to the end, so that the two remaining in the punt would know where they were.

"After Sukuna and his buddy had been fishing for a while, they checked in with each other. Sukuna's buddy had four fish and wanted to swim back to the punt with Sukuna to unload their catch, but Sukuna said, 'You go back. I only have one fish so I'll keep going. Drop off your fish, then come back.'

"While Sukuna's buddy was handing his four fish up to the young men in the punt, they heard people on shore shouting loudly in an agitated, urgent manner, pointing at Sukuna's float jerking violently up and down in the water. When the friends looked for where the float had been, they could no longer find it because by then it was well below the surface.

"The three men swam to Sukuna's last location as quickly as possible. Sukuna's dive buddy swam the fastest, spotting the float several meters below the surface and Sukuna's still body lying on the bottom. Even though the ocean floor was pretty deep for free diving, he dove down and was able to raise Sukuna's heavy body a few meters off the bottom. The second friend was already on his way down and relieved the first rescuer, who had to surface by then for desperately needed air. Likewise, the second friend was relieved by the third friend and in this manner they brought Sukuna's lifeless body to the surface and managed to get it into the punt.

"Nothing was left of Sukuna's left arm but bone, so he must have used it to fight off the shark. His left side, where he must have been wearing the fish he speared, was totally gone. Intestines and guts were found on the line attached to the float."

"Stop, Jack, really. This is gruesome." I declared. "What did they do with the body?"

"Even though it was obvious Sukuna was dead, they felt the right thing to do was take the body to the hospital in Somosomo, where I picked it up two days later just before the funeral began."

"What a story. That is truly sad about Sukuna," Rog said.

"You know, during the eleven months I was spearfishing in Labasa, I lost five friends to shark attacks. All of them were carrying dead fish while they were spearfishing. I always told my friends to surface after each catch and unload the fish in the punt, like I did, but in their eagerness to show off their skill, they resisted taking the time to do this."

I changed the subject. "How's Sofi doing, Jack?"

"This is my opinion, okay."

"Gotcha."

"Sofi is just experiencing growing pains. She's got more freedom than she's ever had and she doesn't quite know what to do with her time. She's in with a crowd that drinks a lot of grog and I think she's unhappy with the direction her life is going right now, so she takes it out on me. Of course, it's true I'm making next to nothing on this fishing boat and I do spend some of the little money I make on liquor, and that pisses Sofi off. But heck, she's pretty irritable all the time now anyway, so I don't go out of my way to be around her a lot, which pisses her off even more. It's sort of a vicious cycle."

"Addictions are so tough on people," I said. "I don't think most people realize that sugar, caffeine and alcohol actually irritate the body and that irritation comes out in the person's personality. Rog and I lived through alcoholism ourselves and I'll just bet that *kava* does the same thing after a while. I hope you're watching how much alcohol you're drinking, Jack."

"Oh, I am. Sofi makes it out to be much more than it is. I just love her to death, though, and I'm sort of waiting for this phase of our lives to play itself out."

Rog chimed in. "I suppose Sofi could get a job here in Savusavu if she wants more money. She's probably never had a formal job before, so that would be a huge step for her."

"I don't see that happening," Jack said, "but I'm not quite sure what will happen in the long run. And that's the hard part—the not knowing."

"Jack, please tell Sofi I miss her and I'm thinking about her and praying for both of you. I know it's hard for her to see us now that we're in the outer bay. And without a phone or VHF contact, there's no way for us to arrange to meet her anywhere. So just let her know that she's in my heart."

"Okay, I will. She's in my heart, too."

With that, we all said our *moce madas* and Jack untied the painter of the borrowed skiff.

"Do come see us again," Rog said as I gave Jack a hug.

"We truly miss you two. I'm sure you know that." I gazed directly into his eyes.

"I do. Thank you." And he was gone.

Organizing the five hundred forty slides I'd taken since our arrival in Fiji became my major project during our Savusavu sojourn. I used a Siro Star 2000, an antiquated manual slide projector that drew very little power. The view screen was eight inches square, which gave me a large image to work with, and there was also a knob for bringing each slide into focus. I could stack no more than twelve slides into the loader or it would jam.

My task was to choose which images to keep, and which ones I wanted to have prints made of for our friends in Viani Bay. Before starting each slide-viewing session, I covered the three portholes in our stateroom with navy blue covers I made with scissors and Velcro from plastic placemats. Then I closed the doors to both the head and the main salon, creating a dark compartment. I sat cross-legged on the bunk for hours at a time, immersed in my project. Although I wished her colors were more vibrantly captured, I was happy with how well six of the thirty-six slides of Glory turned out, especially considering that I had not used an underwater strobe. I knew I'd treasure these slides forever, and hoped the prints would turn out equally well.

Of course, I didn't just sit in the darkened cabin the whole time. One of the highlights of our time in Savusavu was meeting John and Joyce Proctor from Roseburg, Oregon. Pilots of some renown, in 1992 this couple purchased a disabled Grumman amphibious aircraft known as an Albatross. It took five thousand man-hours to restore this former Naval aircraft and convert the interior into a flying, floating home. When we met John and Joyce, they had been on their unique "voyage" almost a year and a half, visiting Mexico, Alaska, Russia, Japan, the Philippines, Australia, New Zealand and now Fiji. They hoped to visit Samoa, Christmas Island and Hawaii before returning to mainland USA.

John and Joyce were as down-to-earth and hospitable as any couple you would ever want to meet. They invited us aboard their floating aircraft which, like *Dreamer,* had all the comforts of home in a compact space: polished hardwood floor, a small bed, bathroom with toilet and shower, refrigerator, stove, small dining area, and a chart table with an easily accessible computer. In addition to being a seasoned pilot and scuba diver, Joyce was an excellent cook, serving us a seafood casserole I've never been able to duplicate, followed by a scrumptious dessert.

John regaled us with stories of his historic flight across Russia in a Cessna 185 Skywagon to promote international friendship through aviation. John left Soviet airspace just as the coup d'état rocked the Soviet Union on August 19, 1991. His adventures during this amazing trip are recounted in his fascinating book *Viktor, Vodka, and Raw Fish*.

Unless the seas were extremely turbulent, landing the Albatross was no problem for Joyce and John. Take-offs, however, were a little more challenging. The day of their departure, we assisted them in our dinghy in getting their anchor line unwrapped from around a coral head. Then we got out of their way, as they revved up their twin engines and utilized most of outer Savusavu Bay to achieve their takeoff.

Several days later, there was an article in *The Fiji Times* about the Proctors, which I saved as a souvenir. When we arrived in Australia a half year later, I contacted them and ordered John's book, which he graciously autographed, thanking us for the great time he and Joyce had on board *Dreamer* on his fiftieth birthday.

Hot, lazy days, complete with beach parties and barbecues, turned into weeks and before we knew it, it was time to head back into Savusavu's inner harbor for the arrival of our friends from California, Buddy and Ruth. The Ellisons arrived six hours earlier than expected, exactly fifteen minutes before the delivery of our brand new, bright yellow dinghy, which we promptly named *Mellow*, short for *Mellow Yellow*.

The timing proved fortuitous in that Buddy, an experienced carpenter, spent the next two days helping Rog to strengthen *Mellow's* floor boards while Ruth and I went shopping in the thriving metropolis of Savusavu.

A few days later, we raised anchor and left outer Savusavu Bay. Trolling with our two-hundred-pound test line, we caught a twenty-two pound yellowfin tuna that provided many tasty meals in the weeks ahead. Of course, we were headed for Vodovodonabolo Bay, which we all now referred to as Glory's Cove.

Chapter 18

LAST ROUND

Our allotted time in Fiji was winding down quickly as *Dreamer* left Savusavu with our guests on board. We would be leaving Fiji ourselves shortly after their three-week visit with us ended.

"We're off, into the wild blue yonder! Well, not quite," I said to Buddy and Ruth as Rog unfurled the large genoa to take advantage of the light breeze. "Actually, our plan is to take you to our favorite hideaways, meet some of our favorite Fijian friends, and do a little snorkeling and scuba diving. First we're going to Vodovodonabolo Bay where we hope you'll be able to experience Glory, the wild fish I told you about in my letters."

"To be perfectly honest, your experiences with this fish are fairly unbelievable," Ruth said. "Being the scuba diving aficionado that he is, Buddy is anxious to see for himself whether this is a fabrication of your imagination!"

"Well, the only problem is that we've been away from Glory's Cove for ten weeks now, and the Fijians spear these giant triggerfish for food, so I'm keeping my fingers crossed, to say the least, that she's still alive. Glory is a legend now in Viani Bay, so I feel confident that no one from that village would harm her. However, people do come to her uninhabited cove from the island of Taveuni, too, so she's always at risk. We'll just have to wait and see when we get there tomorrow afternoon."

"By the way," Ruth added, "Did you warn me that it was going to be this hot?"

"Yep, I told you a couple of times, but it's another one of those things that's difficult to believe until you experience it for yourself."

"I'll say," Ruth replied.

"You can cool off in the water when we get to Glory's Cove. For that matter, you can jump in at Fawn Harbour this evening, but I have to warn you it's a bit muddy. We anchor in the shallow water just outside of the mangrove trees.

Buddy promptly stretched out in the cockpit along the port side, while Ruth took the wheel. I'd sailed with them several times on their Perry 41 in San Francisco Bay, and even with a steady fifteen-knot breeze blowing Buddy would often hunker down for a nap, leaving Ruth to pilot *Mariasha II* to its final destination.

Ruth's one-piece, navy blue bathing suit complimented her short, curvaceous body. Framed by her short, curly brown hair, the relaxed expression on Ruth's suntanned, smooth-complexioned face gave hint to a personality that took life in stride. Her outgoing, helpful nature won her more good friends than I could count on my fingers and toes combined. On the other hand, Ruth did not mince words. She was forthright in speech and you always knew exactly where you stood with her.

Buddy was equally relaxed. Standing about six feet tall, strong and lean but definitely not mean, Buddy was always willing to add a helping hand when it came to home or boat repairs. You didn't always know what Buddy was thinking, though. He had served in Vietnam and although he never talked about it, I sensed that he carried some heavy emotional baggage. But his smile and friendship were as genuine as Ruth's, and together, they entertained many people on board *Mariasha II* and in their Novato, California, home.

Ruth, Rog and I caught up on our mutual friends in the San Francisco Bay area while Buddy continued sawing Zs. Finally, Buddy stirred. "You know," he said, "Ruth and I are seriously considering taking a voyage like yours since we replaced *Mariasha II* and moved aboard our forty-eight-footer, *Annapurna*."

"You two are well-suited for this type of life-style and I think you'll really enjoy yourselves. Do you know much about navigation?" Rog asked.

"Just about nothing," Buddy responded honestly. "I'm hoping you'll teach me and Ruth some of the things we'll need to know."

"Happy to. We have two and a half weeks left together, plenty of time for you to get hands-on experience. How about Morse code? Do you have a ham radio license?"

"Negative."

"Well, I consider that a must for safety purposes," Rog said. "And I can't imagine Ruth existing without staying in touch with all her friends. You'll also need to get a weather fax so that you can keep tabs on the approaching low pressure systems. You'll have to learn all about how and when to change the oil in your diesel engine. We added an extra compressor to ours to help draw down the temperatures in our refrigerator system."

"In exchange for all this help, Ruth and I will pitch in with the cooking on this trip. Don't think you have to do it all, Debby. I remember your fondness for cooking!" Several years back, I had invited thirty guests including Buddy and Ruth to our San Francisco condo for Roger's surprise fiftieth birthday bash. I prepared all the food myself. During the party the casseroles overflowed, filling the kitchen with smoke, and Buddy and Ruth will attest that was the one and only time I ever had them over for a meal!

"I really appreciate that. I've gotten much better at cooking on board *Dreamer*, but it's still not my favorite pastime. I'll prepare breakfast but I'll take you up on your offer for dinners. We can split them fifty-fifty."

"You're on," Ruth added. Ruth and Buddy worked well together in the galley, producing many tasty one-pot meals; they also taught me how to bake macaroni and cheese in my pressure cooker.

When we reached Fawn Harbour, we couldn't resist jumping into the water to cool off. But ascending the ladder fifteen minutes later, we were covered with salt and a thin, almost imperceptible film of dirt.

"Ruth, let me show you a great water-saving method for washing your hair." I filled one of our six gallon buckets half-full of lukewarm water from our tanks. I lowered my head into the bucket. Next, I lathered up with shampoo, working the soap vigorously through my long, blonde hair. But instead of dunking my hair back in the bucket to rinse the soap, I used a two-cup measure to scoop water from the bucket and pour it over my hair and down the cockpit drain, keeping the water in the bucket from getting soapy. In effect, I used the same water twice, and there was still enough left over for Ruth to quickly wash her short brown ringlets.

"Good idea," Ruth said. "Buddy and I are eager to learn all of your little cruising tips for our voyage."

"Well, you'll want to get an inverter installed so you can use equipment like this Food Saver." I pulled my shrink-wrap machine out to demonstrate, taking the filleted yellowfin tuna from the fridge. I took out a roll of shrink-wrap, cut the fillets into individual servings and used the machine to vacuum seal six meals that went into our freezer.

"I don't know whether your freezer on *Annapurna* is powerful enough to withstand the tropical heat. We had ours re-fabricated in New Zealand. Before they worked on it, it only kept cold enough to be a refrigerator. The Kiwis installed stainless steel brine tanks for both the refrigerator and the freezer, and Freon flows through copper piping within the brine tanks to chill each unit."

"Oh, let me start a list in my notebook!"

"Yes, that's what we did when we were getting ready to go cruising," I chuckled, remembering the excitement we felt as we checked each item off of our to-do list.

The next day dawned clear and still, with only enough wind to motor sail again. We arrived at 12:40 p.m., and because I had told Ruth and Buddy that Glory often appeared on the surface as we were lowering our anchor chain, Buddy asked where she was. I was just hoping she was still alive since we'd been gone two and a half months.

As soon as the anchor was securely set, we leaped into the beautiful, clear water with our masks on. Sure enough, about three minutes later I saw Glory swimming along the port side and my heart exploded with joy. Everyone else was off the starboard stern. I called to the others that she was coming their way and they were careful not to splash around or make aggressive moves. As a result, Glory swam near the four of us for about ten minutes while we all remained fairly stationary and just watched her. As usual, I was in total awe of her presence. Ruth and Buddy were duly impressed, agreeing that she was a gorgeous, friendly fish.

About a half hour after we all got out, I saw Glory swimming nearby, so I jumped back in again. I swam away from her and within fifteen seconds she passed nearby on my right. Glory took the lead and I did my best to follow, but she'd gone at least two yards ahead and fairly far below. She kept going deeper until she disappeared altogether. I didn't mind, though, because Glory was alive. Once again, she recognized *Dreamer* and graced all of us with her friendliness. I was ecstatic, actually, and swam to shore where I sat on the beach alone for a while, to fully drink in this miracle once again.

The next day I woke at 3:45 a.m. and got up to do my exercises and meditation without feeling rushed. I knew, or I should say I guessed, that Glory would come around between 6:00 and 6:30, and I wanted to have my meditation completed to spend time with her before Ruth and Buddy got up. I never had to worry about Rog getting up too early! I thought of making banana pancakes, but when I looked outside at around 6:40 to see if Glory had shown up yet, there she was!

It was a gorgeous, still morning. I found an extra loaf of bread in the freezer and fed her. The remoras sucker fishes that live underneath our boat also wanted the bread and lashed out after Glory. It was clear she was afraid, so I got into our *Mellow* with a slice of bread and my mask, snorkel and fins, and detached from *Dreamer*. I fed Glory with my feet dangling over the side. She was not afraid of my feet and swam nearby for each little white chunk floating on the surface.

Mellow drifted ever so slowly into the shallow water, about twelve feet deep. I put on my mask, snorkel and fins and went over the side for what turned out to be my all-time favorite swim with Glory. We went through our checking-each-other-out routine very briefly. Then Glory took the lead and I followed. She took me to a small bommie where one of her siblings and one of her cousins were swimming. Of course, I made this relationship up. I had no idea whether these fish were related or not, but since there were so very few giant triggerfish in Vodovodonabolo Bay, it seemed possible that they could be related. In any event, Glory paused to explore this coral head and the other two triggerfish swam off.

Eventually, she came out of a crevice and turned back toward *Dreamer*, but we swam beyond the boat into the shallow water where we stayed together and played for at least an hour. I was so happy! Glory was cautious whenever I dove down, keeping her distance, but remaining in my vision. However she came near me—very near me sometimes—when I was on the surface.

I owned a Citizen dive watch and finally I glanced at it to find it was 8:20. I'd been with Glory for more than an hour and a half! Reluctantly, I knew I had to return to

Dreamer to cook the pancakes since we had guests aboard, guests who'd been up quite a while by then. Glory was still near me when I terminated our marathon swim together and I felt that she would have loved to continue it.

That swim charged me up so much I kept going all day long until 11:00 p.m. without feeling the slightest bit tired. The next morning, Rog, Buddy and I caught the best tide for scuba diving on Annie's Bommie, out in the middle of Somosomo Strait.

But our time together was swiftly passing. A day later, we took Ruth and Buddy for our last ever Sunday dinner at the Fisher Homestead, immediately after church. Jack and Sofi were supposed to arrive from Savusavu for our last supper with the family, but they didn't show. Still, we had a nice meal with everyone else. I delighted May with several sets of prints, primarily from Sara Fisher's twenty-first birthday party. I also showed her the prints I had made of Glory. For the first time, May seemed slightly impressed, but remained noncommittal to my claim of actually swimming with a wild fish.

I had suggested to Ruth that she might enjoy staying at the Homestead for a few days to really soak in the Fijian culture, but after we left Ruth commented that she would have felt very uncomfortable staying there. I think she might have reacted differently had Sofi and Jack been at the Homestead, and I was hoping and praying that their relationship had improved since I last saw them.

On Monday morning, March 18th, I got up bright and early again. We were about to leave Vodovodonabolo

Bay for our next destination and I wanted to have a little time with my fish after meditation. Glory was waiting for me when I finished my morning routine. I decided to feed her in *Mellow* so I could be closer to her. The highlight of the morning was when Glory swam right up to within a few inches of *Mellow* to get her bread. I wanted to reach out and touch her, but of course, I didn't. While I fed her, I felt that we exchanged the most loving vibrations.

Mellow, Glory and I had drifted some distance away from *Dreamer* by the time Glory's bread was gone. For some reason, she scooted off and although I searched for quite a while, she never re-appeared. Back at *Dreamer*, I told Ruth that Glory had disappeared on me and she replied, "I know. She's been right here."

I went back into the water and this time, my amazing little fish led me in a loop towards the shore, then around to the right towards the coral on the east side of the bay and then back to *Dreamer's* ladder, whereupon she dove down and vanished. But when I got out of the water and toweled off, there she was at the stern again. Unfortunately, I needed to make breakfast before our departure for Qamea Island, so I sent her my love and my gratitude for our friendship before heading below.

We powered from Glory's Cove to Naiviivi Bay on Qamea Island. It was still oppressively hot and we all jumped into the water as soon as the anchor was set. During our stay, Ruth and Buddy treated us to a delicious dinner at the Qamea Beach Club. Rog, Buddy and I did a couple of scuba dives with the resort dive masters while

Jo Kloss, the owner of the resort, kindly allowed Ruth to use one of the bures free of charge during our absence.

We had invited John, Siga, Ella, Alex and Filippe Mitchell, our best Fijian friends in the Naiviivi Bay area, over to our boat for dinner. As luck would have it, the sky poured cats and dogs that night, but they came anyway. The dinner party was a great success. We said a permanent good-bye to the Mitchell family, promising to write each other after *Dreamer* left Fiji.

I was also hoping to see Jack and Sofi reunited and back at the Fisher Homestead before we left, so instead of a side trip to one of our favorite hangouts, Matagi Island, we motor sailed back to Glory's Cove instead. My pet fish did not greet us upon our arrival, and I confess that I worried about her all evening, wondering whether something had happened to her. I was particularly worried that Abu had speared her on purpose, angry because we intended to sell our eight horsepower outboard engine to Jack instead of to him. Rog assured me that Abu would never spear Glory; clearly he loved her and had written such a beautiful song about her.

When she showed up early Saturday morning, I was thrilled. I had a great time feeding her but did not swim with her.

Rog and I took *Mellow* into Viani Bay by ourselves the next day, to say good-bye to Jack and Sofi and whoever else was around. I kept putting off our departure; possibly because I feared Jack and Sofi wouldn't be there and possibly because I didn't want to have to say good-bye. I thought the world of them and for the first time on our voyage, I truly dreaded a farewell.

When Ruth and Buddy went into the water, Glory showed up almost immediately. I had a great time watching her swim back and forth, very close to them; then swim away and back again. Ruth asked, "Aren't you coming in, Deb?" But I was having too much fun watching from the stern, as Glory befriended our friends. She was such a brave little fish.

After Glory finally swam away, Rog and I sped off for Viani Bay. Reaching the familiar beach at the foot of the Homestead property, I was overjoyed to hear my dear friend Sofi's voice as she ran down the lawn. I easily picked up her tiny frame and whirled her around.

"Sofi, Sofi, it's so good to see you. How is everyone, and especially, how are you and Jack? Are you home for good, I hope?"

"We fine, and yes, Jack agree to come home. Hard to believe, but he swallow pride and agree to come back. Loi must go back to school, but we not have enough money to send her. We think we do better here, to take people over to Taveuni for shopping and not spending money like we do in Savusavu."

I was delighted.

"We can give you some money for Loi's school, too," Rog said and I gave him a grateful look.

"Thank you so much, Roger. That be a big help for us, no matter how much you give. I saw all photos you give to May, and 'Ode To Glory' all typed up with Abu and Andrea's photo. Very special. We hung it on wall in living room. We better go to house now. Jack waits for you, too."

Arm in arm we walked up the gorgeous lawn together for the last time. My heart was very heavy. As soon as we approached the wooden house, we saw Jack emerge onto the little porch, waving and calling out to us, "*Bula*, my dear friends. *Bula*. *Bula*."

I ran up the steps, threw my arms around him and cried out, "Oh Jack, it's so good to see you and Sofi back home where you belong."

"Yes, and why do you have to leave us?"

"You know we cannot stay forever. We have to check out of Fiji by May 8th at the very latest. You were with us when your chief said we could stay no more than nine months. Also, Rog has some things he wants to do in both Savusavu and Suva before we leave."

"To us, you are part of our family. We don't want to see you go. But I have a few things to do in Savusavu myself, such as telling the owners of the fishing boat that I've decided to stay here in Viani Bay after all. Can I hitch a ride with you?"

"Yes, be ready by 7:30 tomorrow morning. We're going to make the trip in one day this time."

"Okay, I'll be there."

"Well, I do believe I smell Sofi or Andrea's scones. Am I right about that?"

"Yes, I make them. I make them," Sofi appeared, all excited. "They very special ones for you and Roger. Here they are and some iced tea, too. Please, sit down and have some now."

This was such a bittersweet day. I rejoiced at seeing my dear friends back home, together and sober, both of them looking so happy. But the thought that I might never ever see them again was tearing away at my heartstrings. By the time we finished the scones, and they tasted particularly delicious that afternoon, it was nearly 4:00.

Sofi told me to close my eyes and when I opened them, there on the table were two items that she'd made for me, both woven from coconut fronds: a beautiful basket for fruits and a small covered container, almost the shape of a little teapot with a lid, to hold pieces of paper written with the names of friends in need of prayers. Sofi disappeared again and re-emerged with a shell necklace and a pair of delicate matching earrings for me. Rog did not receive any gifts that day but he's never forgotten the frangipani lei Andrea made for his fifty-seventh birthday.

"Rog, I want to spend as much time as possible with Sofi and Jack. If Jack will bring me back before it gets dark, would you be willing to go back to *Dreamer* by yourself and help Buddy and Ruth get some dinner together?"

So Jack walked Rog back down to the beach and helped him get our new, larger and heavier dinghy back into the water. In the meantime, Sofi and I sat out on the lawn overlooking Viani Bay with the spine of Taveuni Island outlined against the fading blue sky on the far side of Somosomo Strait. We talked on and on, reminiscing about our many, many adventures together. From time to time, tears streamed down our cheeks as we simultaneously laughed and cried. We exchanged our contact information, promising to write to one another forever.

I told her that I'd sign some travelers' checks for Loi's next semester at school and give them to Jack before he left *Dreamer*, asking if she felt confident that he wouldn't spend the money in Savusavu.

"Yes," she said. "Give money to Jack. He bring back to Viani Bay in few days and give checks to bank in Waiyevo. Then we pay for school."

"Good. I'm glad that you trust each other again. You just had to go through some hard times. We all have ups and downs to grow through and learn from."

We talked about God in our lives. I shared three stories of times when I was consciously aware that God was protecting Rog and me during our voyage. The first happened in French Polynesia, as we were approaching Papeete at night. I was on watch from midnight to 4:00 a.m. and Rog cautioned me to slow down if the wind picked up, because he didn't want to go into the unfamiliar harbor in the dark. At about 2:00 in the morning, the wind picked up dramatically, so I decided to roll up the genoa and woke Rog up to help me.

Before coming into the cockpit, he kept staring at the chart and then looking forward to see where we were going. Annoyed, I said, "You don't have to navigate. I'm heading exactly where you told me to head. Now please, just help me furl the sail so you can go back to sleep."

Actually, I had misunderstood Roger's directions. I thought he told me to head straight for the lighthouse beacon, but in fact there was a reef between *Dreamer* and that beacon. Had the wind not come up, causing me to awaken Rog, I would have put *Dreamer* right on the reef. As it was, we furled the headsail and corrected our heading. Then Rog went back to sleep and the wind promptly died right back down!

I was again on night watch during a five-day passage to the Tuamotu Atolls, when I heard many birds squawking overhead. In a gesture of welcome, I called, "Come land on *Dreamer* and take a load off your wings." Instead they kept screeching until finally I looked up into the sky behind me. Even though it was the middle of the night, I could make out a truly huge, black squall approaching. I headed the boat off, letting out both sails to ease the effect of the stronger winds on the rigging, the helm and the heel of the boat.

I had just enough time to make these corrections before the forty-knot winds hit us. *Dreamer* was on a reach, with the wind striking about sixty degrees aft of the bow, and while it still took skill to sail the boat, it was much easier to handle the heavy winds on a reach than on the previous beat. The squall lasted about twenty minutes and when it ended, the birds returned. Their pleasant chirping was sweet music to my ears, indeed. It was as if they were saying, "You made it, and we were watching out for you while you were riding it out."

Finally, I told Sofi about the time when we left Nelson, New Zealand, to sail to Fiji the second time. All the other cruisers we knew had left New Zealand approximately two months earlier, and snow was already on the peaks in Abel Tasman National Park as we departed. Seven hours later, we were heading up the Tasman Sea when Rog happened to touch the stern pulpit and the binnacle at the same time. Both were made of polished stainless steel and Rog was startled to feel a light electrical current coursing through his body.

He reacted quickly, fearing for the integrity of our through hull fittings. First, we hove to in order to steady the motion of the boat in the twenty-five-knot winds. Next, Rog quickly located his multimeter and began the hour-long job of tracking down two electrical shorts. Our oldest solar panel was the main culprit, with the starboard wind generator adding to the charge. We had to cut and tape the wire from the solar panel and prevent the wind generator fan from spinning by tying it off, no easy job in the moderately strong wind.

Undetected, that electrical short could have caused our brass through hull fittings to disintegrate. With a ten-thousand-pound keel, one or more holes in the bottom of a boat generally results in it sinking. In the cold waters of the Tasman Sea that time of the year, I doubt we would have survived a twenty-mile swim back to New Zealand. We might have survived only if we managed to deploy our life raft in time, a feat not accomplished by the crew of *Quartermaster* during The Queen's Birthday Storm.

I'd been gazing out toward the water, but turned to face Sofi and said, "I have always been fond of the expression, 'A coincidence is a miracle in which God wishes to remain anonymous'. Surely Roger's touching our binnacle and our stern pulpit simultaneously was a coincidence, or should I say a miracle!"

"I wish God would create miracle right now so that you do not leave us."

"Me too," I replied. "Always remember, my darling Sofi, to find your happiness inside of yourself. That is where God dwells, and if you are very quiet, you can feel joy and peace in your heart. You are responsible for your own decisions and your own happiness. No one can take these things away from you unless you let them. Do you understand what I'm saying, my dearest friend?"

We gave each other a long hug, sitting there on the lawn as the sun sank low in the sky. It was time for me to leave.

"Dearest Sofi, I will write to you, but you have to promise to answer my letters. I love you very much."

"Yes, yes, of course I write. My love for you very big, too."

We both cried as we hugged and kissed good-bye. Sofi stayed at the Homestead and Jack walked me down to his punt on the shore. The sun was setting behind the western hills curving around Viani Bay. The sky was magnificent with orange and pink deepening into gold and purple as Jack took a longer route out of the bay, hugging the western shoreline, even though Glory's Cove was to the east.

"Why does life deal us these sad, sad good-byes, Jack?"

I was crying uncontrollably now. He put his arm around me as he steered the boat with his other hand.

"You have been just like family to us. You're always welcome here whenever you can come, Debby. We love you and Roger so very much for the wonderful times we've shared together and for all of your loving ways."

"But Jack, you know that the odds are we will never be able to come back."

"Never say never," he replied. "That's what you told Sofi one day, and she always remembers that when I say we might never get married because my wife won't give me a divorce. It gives us a lot of hope."

Jack headed east and we left Viani Bay as darkness surrounded us. When we rounded the outer reef and entered into Vodovodonabolo Bay, we could see *Dreamer's* cabin lights glowing through her portholes and out through the companionway. I held tightly onto the bag containing all the treasures Sofi had given me as I stepped aboard *Dreamer* and waved good-bye to Jack.

"Well, here comes our wayward wanderer now," Roger joked, trying to cheer me up. "We saved some dinner for you."

Everyone could clearly see I'd been crying. I had a bite or two, then said I had to go to bed so I could get up early and say good-bye to Glory. *"Oh my, another good-bye,"* I thought before heading for the bunk.

Glory's behavior the next morning truly amazed me, and I'll never forget it. I got up very early, at about 3:45 a.m., inexplicably in an excellent frame of mind. When I finished meditating, Glory was right there waiting for me. I went below and retrieved two slices of bread, which I fed to her lovingly. Then I took down some laundry and did a few other little outdoor chores, getting ready to depart.

In the meantime, Glory kept swimming back and forth along the starboard side of the boat, watching me. She had this peculiar way of swimming with her body slightly tilted so that her eye, whichever one was towards the boat, could look up at me. I finally stopped puttering and watched her, realizing this was really good-bye for Glory, too—we weren't ever coming back this time. I felt certain that Glory knew we were leaving because she kept up her vigil for an hour and a half, even after Rog started up the engine. When she finally turned and swam away, I looked up and saw Jack's boat just rounding the reef. Glory must have felt the vibrations and knew it was time for her to let me go. Tears welled up in my eyes, thinking about my faithful little friend swimming back and forth, back and forth, not wanting our special relationship to end.

Jack arrived with Abu at the helm and Aseta on board to say good-bye. When Rog handed Aseta the machine screws, washers and nuts he had bought for her in Savusavu for her dining room chairs, she broke down in tears, saying that in all these years no one had taken the time to locate hardware to fix her ailing chairs. Aseta was such a lovely woman, truly gorgeous from the inside out. She'd brought us kasava and fruit for our trip. Jack brought coconut oil and a large basket full of fruit from May, plus lots of bananas and other food as well.

In fact, during the sixteen days Ruth and Buddy were on board, we never once had to go to a market after our initial food shopping in Savusavu and we always had fresh produce: Chris and Sia Fisher brought us custard apples; Bob and Sotia Covert brought heaps of produce including fresh spinach, pawpaws, pineapples, avocados, etc.; John and Siga Mitchell gave us green peppers, tomatoes, a cabbage and some fruit. We were well provided for by the generosity of our Fijian friends.

Jack came aboard *Dreamer* for his ride to Savusavu. After saying our good-byes to Aseta and Abu, we weighed anchor at 7:45 a.m. I put the gifts of food away and worked on breakfast to keep myself busy. But after breakfast, I headed into our bunk with my six favorite photos of Glory and proceeded to cry my heart out. I couldn't write to Glory like I could to Sofi. This good-bye was truly final.

I felt the deepest sadness. In order to prevent that huge feeling of emptiness from lodging permanently in my heart, I grabbed my *On Deck Log* and wrote: "Well, God, I miss Glory, but I thank You from the bottom of my heart for manifesting Thyself unto me in the form of this beautiful, courageous, intelligent and loving fish. And thank You for the photos, also. I will never forget her, and please, God, let me never, ever forget You or take You for granted. I want to think of You day and night, night and day. Please, please help me to do this, for I am a slow learner and need to be reminded constantly. Glory was a wonderful way to show me how very much You love me, and she will live on in my heart forever. Thank You, God."

EPILOGUE

FROM FIN TO FUR

In November, 1997, I attended a week-long retreat in Melbourne, Australia with Mata Amritanandamayi, known as the Hugging Saint. Amma travels the world every year, making herself available to her millions of devotees, so it's been easy for me to visit with her once a year. She is an authentic avatar. I believe that swimming with Glory in 1995 and 1996 foreshadowed my acquaintance with her love, her teachings and her blessings.

In March, 1998, Buddy and Ruth Ellison left Acapulco, Mexico, on their forty-eight-foot Hans Christian center cockpit motorsailer, *Annapurna*, to start a circumnavigation that they successfully completed nine years later in April, 2007. They now live in southern California and Ruth is currently writing a book about their voyage.

Sofi and I have successfully kept in touch via letters exchanged approximately once a year, so I've been able to keep up with the lives of some of the Fijians in Viani Bay. Sofi's Auntie in Raviravi Village died in 2001, five years after Sofi, Loi and I took the bus trip to visit Sofi's original home. Aseta Fisher moved to New Zealand to be with family members who had moved there earlier. May Fisher died in 2007 at the age of ninety-two, and Jack and Sofi were forced to move out of the Homestead. They chose a plot of land close to the water, but not far from the Homestead, for their new *bure*. Loi gave birth to a daughter, Tiare Elizabeth, who is being raised by Jack and Sofi. And best of all, Jack finally obtained a divorce from his first wife and on March 11, 2011, Jack and Sofi were officially married.

Rog and I sold *Dreamer* and moved to the mountains of central Colorado in February of 2000. Relaxed and radiant, I was eager to share the God-spark within me with all the new people I met in our artistic, high mountain valley community. I knew that God is not separate from us; we are the microcosm and God is the macrocosm. We are One. By allowing the God Energy and Consciousness to flow through us, unimpeded by fears or desires, we can transmit God's wondrous qualities throughout the world and thus help heal our planet. Being patient, tolerant, loving, kind and forgiving of all beings, knowing that everyone including ourselves is exactly where we are meant to be on life's journey, is also helpful in emanating peaceful vibrations.

As more than a decade of living in Colorado passed, I so over-extended myself that my inner Light grew dim, in direct ratio to my becoming more and more attached to the various things I was doing. I allowed the daily distractions of my lifestyle to prevent me from concentrating more fully on my soul essence. In other words, I became a human doing instead of a human being.

Just as God came to me in the form of Glory during our voyage, She came again to save me from my ego, this time in the form of my beloved cat Boots. On Valentine's Day of 2011, I clearly received a message from my furry friend during my regular morning meditation, telling me I was wearing him out with my constant activity. He added that I needed to slow down and simplify my life; reconnect with the peace, love and joy of my inner being no matter what I was doing; try to live one moment at a time; trust God totally; and in the midst of activity, remember always to be grateful.

Although sometimes difficult to achieve, I have taken this message to heart. I want to share it with all who read this book so that you, too, might be reminded to slow down, take the time daily to meditate, and remember Who You Are.

ABOUT THE AUTHOR

Photo by Karen Campbell
www.mksphotovideo.com

Debby Cason refers to herself as the Girl Friday of Life. At the age of ten, she learned how to sail. At twelve, she won first place in the Eastern Long Island Regatta and second place in the Shelter Island Yacht Club Summer Race Series in the "Wood Pussy" class.

As an adult, she has dabbled in writing, singing, acting, painting, hiking, skiing, sailing, scuba diving, skydiving, bungee jumping, traveling and photography. Amongst her various money-earning skills, she claims the following roles: secretary, bookkeeper, stockbroker, bank teller, waitress, school bus driver, square dance instructor and assistant manager of a secondhand boutique. Debby continues to enjoy the smorgasbord of life with joy and enthusiasm. *Swimming With Glory* is her first effort at authorship.

Color photos of Roger and Debby's visit to Fiji can be found on the website, www.swimmingwithglory.com. They are also posted on facebook.com/ SwimmingWithGlory.

Debby has a blog at http://SailingSailingBlog.com in which she recounts many sailing adventures and much know-how, accompanied by gorgeous color photos. You can subscribe to her blog by typing in your email address in the Email Subscription box on the right of the home page.

Additional copies of *Swimming With Glory* can be obtained on the website or by emailing Debby at debbycason@rockyhi.net. She welcomes all comments from readers.

To view Erwin Kodiat's underwater photos or to go scuba diving in Indonesia, visit Erwin's website, www.d-scubaclub.com.

PREPARING *DREAMER* FOR OUR VOYAGE

by Roger Cason

(The following is intended to be a list of the significant preparations for our voyage; however, there probably are some items unintentionally omitted. Further, your voyage may well require different preparations than ours did. Therefore, you need to use your own judgment in your voyage preparations and should not just rely on the comments shown below.)

The first step we took in preparation for our planned ocean voyage was to acquire a suitable open ocean cruising sailboat. We had a list of necessary characteristics we were looking for in a cruising sailboat and must have looked at every used boat for sale in the San Francisco Bay area. Since I was still working at the time, Debby took over the task of trouping from yacht broker to yacht broker and marina to marina looking at the boats for sale. In every case we discovered a fatal flaw in the offered boat until one day Debby came home all enthused about a Passport 40 sailboat she had discovered for sale at the Brickyard Cove Marina in Richmond, California.

We both inspected the boat and were mighty impressed. She was a Robert Perry designed ocean cruising boat and met many of our requirements. She had been very well maintained and hardly used at all. Her biggest defect was her price. I finally concluded that although she met almost all of our requirements she was too expensive and we could not afford to buy her. Debby took this solemn pronouncement very poorly and at the conclusion of a long statement of frustration said, "That's it. I refuse to look anymore. I found us the perfect boat and you say we can't buy it. If you want to go cruising, you find the boat." This might not be a perfect translation of what she actually said, but it comes pretty darn close.

Faced with a more than unhappy wife I did what any sane "wanting to remain married male" would do. I completely capitulated and within about a week we were the proud owners of the Passport 40 sailboat we would name *Dreamer*.

We had her surveyed by a highly recommended surveyor and he gave her basically a no problem report. About a year and a half later, however, we discovered a problem with the attachment of the chain plates for the upper and lower shrouds to the hull of the boat. Basically, the attachment was pulling away from the hull. We had that repaired together with a few more modifications at a price of about $10,000. We later found out that the problem we discovered was not atypical with the Passport 40s.

A good philosophy for outfitting a cruising boat is redundancy. The twenty-four-hour, day-in-day-out sailing a cruising sailboat does is far tougher on the gear than periodic day sailing. You do not need the knowledge to fix everything yourself as you will most likely be able to find another cruiser who does have the knowledge. You do need to have on board spares to fix what breaks and for sure, things will break. We carried a spare starter motor and alternators and, of course, they were never needed. We did not carry a spare anchor windless and ours did fail. Fortunately, we were in Thailand and able to get it fixed after a lot of hassle caused by language issues. Their English was better than my Thai, but not by much.

Other things we did to convert a boat well equipped for bay and onshore cruising into a boat well equipped for blue water cruising are described below:

1. Your blue water boat should have a diesel engine. There are various reasons for diesel over gas including safety (diesel fuel is much harder to set on fire or explode than is gas), engine reliability and fuel availability. We were in many places where diesel was plentiful and gas very hard to find.

2. If you are not familiar with diesel engines you should consider taking a mini diesel engine course. Learn such things as how to change the oil, bleed air out of the fuel system, change fuel filters, change injectors and the like. Debby and I did all of our oil changes and had to bleed the air several times.

3. While we liked *Dreamer* a lot at the time of purchase, we did replace the main sail with a fully battened main, added a new genoa and converted the reefing system to a slab system operated from the cockpit. We also replaced the roller furling system with a more robust Harken system.

4. Further, after our accidental gibe while approaching San Diego, we improved her preventer system by running a line from the cockpit to a snatch block attached to the forward mooring cleat and back to the aft end of the boom on both the port and starboard sides. When running downwind we were able to tighten up on the leeward line and cleat it to a cockpit cleat. This was enough to prevent the boom from crashing over if the wind got forward of the main.

5. *Dreamer* had a lot of exterior teak, which looked really smart when varnished. The two of us could barely keep her looking fine in the San Francisco Bay area, but to do so in the tropics would be an impossible task. The answer is to place several fresh layers of varnish over the varnish already there and to then apply two more coats of marine epoxy paint. The epoxy paint will last for several years while the varnish will last for only several months.

6. Install a ham radio and get a ham radio general license. Debby and I actually had advanced licenses which are a help but not necessary. *Dreamer* also

had a single side band (SSB) marine radio, which I would rate as not absolutely necessary but sure nice. If forced to choose between a marine SSB or Ham radio, I would pick the Ham. This is admittedly a personal choice. It is difficult to access the ham bands with a SSB radio while a HAM radio can easily access the SSB bands. My recollection is that such dual access is not in conformance with the FCC rules and regs, but in an emergency, who cares. There are many HAM radio marine nets, which supply a wealth of very helpful info such as weather conditions and port entry procedures.

7. You should have something to help you forecast weather. We had a Furuno weather fax machine on *Dreamer*, which worked really well.

8. I do not believe you need to learn celestial navigation. Rather, install a good hard-wired GPS unit and also acquire a hand held GPS, powered by its own batteries. Store the hand held in a safe place and store its batteries separately. That way, if you go through a big lightning storm (you will at some time in the tropics) and take a hit or near hit, you will not fry both units.

9. And speaking of lightning storms, do something to really ground your boat well. *Dreamer* already had good grounding, but we added two ten-foot-long insulated copper battery cables (I think 00 gauge) and attached each one to an upper shroud with

hose clamps. At the other end of the cable we attached a zinc anode and partially taped the anode so it would not scratch the hull. If it looked like a lightning storm was approaching, we would throw the leeward side cable into the water. It may have been God's will, but we never took a strike in about eight years in the tropics including two crossings of the equator and time spent in the Singapore/Malaysia area. We were threatened several times, but never hit. We were anchored in a bay near Brisbane when a big lightning storm came through and zapped a nearby powerboat. The boat had gas engines with fuel injection and the lightning took out the fuel injection pumps and VHF radio. They needed to be towed back into port.

10. Install a radar reflector high up on the mast. Remember, fiberglass does not reflect radar waves.

11. We installed a masthead tricolor light with a strobe on *Dreamer* and were glad we did.

12. Install a life raft. The raft should have a cover, a double bottom and include survival stores such as flares, water, food, fishing gear and the like. The raft should be set-up so that it is firmly attached to the boat when launched. Think hard about how you would launch the raft in storm conditions. We never had to and have not regretted that particular lack of experience. My personal opinion is that getting into a life raft in storm conditions is a very hazardous procedure. I would recommend not even

trying to board the raft unless the boat is already sinking. We are aware of several cases where boats were found damaged but afloat with an empty life raft still attached, but no one in it.

13. Purchase an EPIRB (Emergency Position-Indicating Radio Beacon). Once again, we hope you will never need one.

14. Self-steering vane. We installed a Monitor wind vane and it was one of our best investments. There is a short period of learning how best to use it, but once that is mastered it steers the boat very well. I would say we used the Monitor at least ninety percent of the time we were cruising. We've used it dead downwind with the genoa polled out in twenty-five knots of wind as well as going to weather. A human can steer a bit better when he/she is rested, but after that the vane has it all over hand steering. It doesn't get tired, need to go to the head, eat or any of the other things humans do. The only breakage we had with the vane was the control lines fraying and preventive maintenance cured that problem. Install the vane so that all of the control lines are easily accessible as they can fray over time and will need to be replaced.

15. We also had an electronic power steerer, which we used primarily while under power.

16. Install solar panels to help keep your batteries charged. We started out with four panels mounted

to the outside of the lifelines by the cockpit. We knew there was a chance a wave would take them out and after about four years of cruising it happened. We then had an arch installed over the stern and mounted three panels on it. The arch also had a lifting arrangement for raising and lowering the outboard to and from the dingy, which was much safer and easier on the Captain's back than our earlier manual method. An added convenience provided by the arch--it was the perfect place to hang large clusters of bananas!

17. We did have wind generators, but ours were not very helpful and we traded them as partial payment for a new radar in Australia. Perhaps they are made better now.

18. We replaced the standard lead acid batteries with gel cells and added two additional gel cells to run the anchor windless and one additional gel cell as an independent engine start battery. Gel cells are more expensive but they are completely maintenance free, will not leak if tipped over, are not damaged too much if drawn down and take a large charge quickly. We believe there is no such thing as too many batteries on a cruising sailboat.

19. We installed a drop-leaf table in the cockpit and loved it. If your boat does not have a cockpit table, please get one. We ate most of our meals on it when weather allowed.

20. You will need a diesel fuel filter to filter out the miscellaneous bits and pieces that come with third world diesel. Ours was aluminum, about three inches in diameter, about eight inches high for the main body and another three inches for the outlet, had three filters inside including a water filter and a one-inch outlet at the bottom. It also had plastic caps for the top and bottom for storage. It worked great. Every liter of fuel we poured into *Dreamer's* tanks went through the filter. Some of that fuel was far less than clean.

21. When we purchased *Dreamer* we thought her refrigeration was a bit weak, but we did not realize that in a tropical environment it was basically useless. While in New Zealand we had the entire system torn out and replaced with new insulation, stainless steel refrigerator/freezer units and a new engine driven compressor. With the new unit we ran the engine one hour a day in the tropics and all worked perfectly.

22. At the same time, we had an additional alternator of 160 amps installed and after a bit of redo regarding the alternator belt, it too worked perfectly so that with the same one hour a day run time, all of our batteries would be fully charged in addition to cooling the brine tanks for the refrigerator and freezer.

23. We needed a bit more storage space so we installed nets in the main cabin to hold additional food.

24. If you have a passion for scuba diving you will need a dive compressor. Ours was heavy, slow and noisy, but it enabled us to dive in remote beautiful areas we would have otherwise missed out on.

25. One of our most important tools was a banding tool, together with some stainless steel strapping material. We carried both ¾" and 1" stainless steel strips. The vang fitting at the base of our mast failed and we were able to fix it while underway with the banding tool. We fixed it so well that we went two years before performing a more permanent fix. Later, the fitting on the boom end of the vang failed, and we were again able to jury rig a fix with the banding tool. GET ONE!!

26. Main Anchors

    • *Dreamer's* main anchor at the start was a 45# CQR type, together with three hundred feet of high-test chain. I think the chain had a working load rating of four thousand pounds. We have anchored in sixty feet of water with that rig, but not in strong wind conditions.
    • We also purchased two Fortress aluminum anchors which were in the Danforth style, but lighter than a Danforth anchor, with very good holding power. For each of these anchors we had twenty feet of chain and

about three hundred feet of ¾ inch nylon line.

- While in Australia we upgraded the 45# CQR type to a 65# CQR type.
- We had stainless steel swivels for each of the anchor lines/chain.
- We replaced the swivel on the main chain each year once we read that after being submerged for a lengthy period of time, stainless steel will begin to corrode internally and lose its strength. We did not know how long it took, but we did know that we once anchored in the same spot for seven weeks and that led us to the replace the main chain swivel every year plan.

27. This anchor inventory worked very well for us; however, we did drag once shortly after we started using the 65# anchor. We were in a large bay in Australia which had a sandy bottom. We were in less than thirty feet of water and did our normal routine of backing down the boat to set the anchor with no problems. However, at about 2:30 in the morning we both awoke as we felt *Dreamer's* keel bumping on the bottom. Up on deck we went to discover we had dragged about a half mile and were in shallow water on a falling tide. We quickly put our two Fortress anchors in our dingy and brought them away from the port side of *Dreamer* as far as we could, brought the two anchor lines back to *Dreamer* and attached one to the stern and one to the bow. We put a lot of tension on each

line using our winches and tried to power off with no joy. We went back to an uncomfortable sleep with *Dreamer* lying pretty much on her side. When we awoke up at 7:00 a.m., *Dreamer* was floating normally, so we fired up the engine, pulled up the bow anchor, the two side anchors and powered back to where we had originally anchored. We discovered that the new bow anchor had impaled a beer can leaving only about two inches of the tip of the anchor exposed. No wonder we dragged anchor and we never did again.

28. Be sure to bring along a Polaroid camera. These are a huge hit with the villagers. You will have the kids and their mothers lined up to get their pictures taken.

29. We also stocked *Dreamer* with gifts for the villagers. Such items as pens, colored pencils, crayons, notebooks, coloring books, T-shirts with *Dreamer's* picture, audio cassette tapes and the like. In many cases the villagers would give us fresh food in return. We also had plastic beach balls of planet Earth as seen from our satellites, which were a big hit.

30. We installed a hydraulic backstay adjuster. This allowed us to adjust the tension on the backstay depending on the conditions. More importantly, it allowed us to release the tension while at anchor.

31. We purchased a Food Saver vacuum packer and it worked great. We used it for all sorts of things. The most obvious was to vacuum pack food, especially food to be frozen. It virtually eliminated freezer burn. But also, I would use it to pack spare engine parts to prevent corrosion and valuable papers, including travelers checks, to prevent mildew.

32. You will need an inverter to be able to run all of those AC toys you cannot live without. Computers, printers, and the above-mentioned Food Saver are examples. Remember though, you will be converting 12v to 110v so the amperage draw from your batteries will be about ten times what the 110v appliance will draw at 110v. That pretty much eliminates a regular hair dryer, for example, as it would draw about 120 amps from your batteries.

33. *Dreamer's* engine was in the main cabin with the oil dipstick on the port side. That was okay for checking the oil, but awkward for changing the oil due to lack of space on that side of the engine. While in New Zealand we had our engine mechanic remove the oil pan, attach an elbow fitting to the bottom of the pan, attach a hose to that fitting and a hand operated oil pump to the hose. The pump was hooked to the starboard side of the engine compartment and we were in business for easy oil changes.

34. Converting *Dreamer* to a cutter rig was not the last change we made, but it was one of the best. While

in New Zealand for her first trip, *Dreamer* received an inner forestay, new staysail and running backstays. What a difference. We wondered how we had survived without them. The running backstays really stiffened up the rig and sharply reduced the pumping of the mast when going to weather in heavy seas. The staysail gave us further options in sail selection. For example, on our third and last trip to New Zealand we were hard on the wind for ten days in winds up to thirty-eight knots. We ended up with three reefs in the main, just the staysail up and the weather side running backstay quite tight. The boat behaved beautifully and the mast was solid. That is not to say it was a comfortable trip, but it was a safe trip and we were moving forward, just not directly toward Nelson, NZ, which was our destination. We obviously made it, as here I am now writing this from Colorado.

35. We were initially concerned about the ability of the two of us handling running backstays. Fellow cruisers and the yard where the work was done assured us it would not be that big a deal and they were right! Yes, the new rig was a little harder to handle while tacking, but we were quickly able to do it with ease. Now, if we were short tacking by ourselves in San Francisco Bay's twenty-five to thirty knot summer breeze, I might give you a different answer. But when you tack two times in twenty-four hours, it was not a problem. So our advice is if you are going cruising, go for a cutter rig with running backs.

36. There were two heavy weather additions we made to *Dreamer* we never had to use. These were a parachute to be deployed from the bow and drogue lines to be deployed from the stern.

- As to the first, we purchased a parachute about six feet in diameter and rigged it to three hundred feet of ¾ inch nylon line which we planned to deploy from a bow mooring cleat. Also as part this arrangement was another three hundred foot section of ¾ inch nylon line with an eye spliced around a thimble. The plan was to attach a snatch block to the end of this line with the bow line running through the block. This last line would then be run back to a cockpit winch and used to adjust the angle of the boat to the waves.

- We both questioned our ability to deploy this system in storm conditions. Imagine yourself up on the bow in say fifty knots of wind and big seas trying to launch the parachute with the bow going under with each wave. Assuming you manage this feat without also launching yourself, you then have to attach the snatch block while your partner gets ready to haul in on the snatch block line.

- We tried a practice effort near San Miguel Island, an infamous area of heavy wind near Point Conception in California, and had just so-

so success. We did take the system with us and prayed that we would never feel the need to use it and our prayers were answered.

- The second system was much easier to deploy. The plan was to stream the two lines mentioned above from the stern of *Dreamer* (no parachute needed here) to slow her down while running downwind in breaking seas, the hope being that this would prevent a pitch pole at the bottom of the wave. We believed that this system was quite usable and maybe even helpful. Once again, we never felt the need to launch this system.

If you can't sail to Fiji, there are three resorts we enjoyed visiting from 1994 to 1996: the Jean-Michel Cousteau Resort in Savusavu, the Matangi Island Resort on Matangi Island and the Qamea Beach Club on Qamea Island. In addition, we recently learned of the newly established Rainbow Reef Resort, which is located two bays northeast of Vodovodonabolo Bay.

GLOSSARY FOR GOD

The Alpha and The Omega. The All in All; the Beginning and the End.

Nature. The physical force regarded as causing and regulating the phenomena of the physical world collectively.

Consciousness. A state of being characterized by thought, will, design or perception; awareness.

Energy. The capacity to act or be active.

Creator. One that creates, usually by bringing something new or original into being.

Creation. The bringing into existence of the universes, especially when regarded as an act of God.

Omniscient. Having infinite awareness, understanding and insight.

Omnipotent. Having unlimited power; able to do anything.

Omnipresent. Present in all things at all times.

Oneness. The quality or state or fact of being one in number, though comprised of two or more

parts: singleness; integrity, wholeness;
harmony; sameness, identity; unity, union.

QUALITIES OF GOD

From the Teachings of Paramahansa Yogananda

Love
Light
Sound
Intelligence, Wisdom
Peace
Bliss
Beauty

CONTEMPLATION: GOD IS

ENGLISH PRONUNCIATION
OF FIJIAN SPELLING

a = a as in father

ai = i as in line

b = mb as in bula = mbula

c = th as in moce = mothe

d = nd as in Vodovodonabolo =
Vondovondonambolo (use this
spelling to find on Internet)

e = e as in they

g = ng as in sega no leqa =
senga na lengga

i = i as in machine

o = o as in go

q = ngg as in sega na leqa =
senga na lengga

u = u as in rule

GLOSSARY OF FIJIAN WORDS
AND PHRASES

Au damoni iko. I love you.

Bilo. Individual kava bowl made from half of interior coconut shell.

Bula. Typical Fijian greeting meaning hello or welcome to our home.

Bure. A Fijian dwelling.

Caka caka. Work.

Cumudamu. Giant triggerfish.

Grog. Fijian nickname for kava.

Kailoma. Half Fijian, half European.

Kata kata. Hot.

Kava. Mildly narcotic beverage made by pulverizing yaqona roots.

Lako i sili. Go and take your bath.

Lako mai. Come here.

Lovo. A pit dug into the earth and used as an oven.

Meda marau. Be happy.

Meke. Fijian dance, using upper body and hands to tell a story. Dancers remain seated on the ground.

Moce mada. Good-bye until later.

Moce. Good-bye.

Na kana maleka na kakana. The food is delicious.

Ni sa bula. Good day or hello.

Ni sa yandra. Good morning.

O cei na vale lailai?   Where is the bathroom?

Qai raice iko tale.   See you later.

Sega na leqa.   No worries; often used to say you're welcome.

Sulu.   A wraparound skirt worn as formal attire by Fijian men.

Tanoa.   Large community kava bowl.

Tapa cloth.   Fabric made by pounding the bark of the mulberry bush.

Vavalangi.   Caucasian person of Anglo descent.

Vinaka na vakayaqataka.   You're welcome.

Vinaka vaka levu.   Thank you very much.

Vinaka.   Thank you.

Walu.   Mild-flavored fish for eating, generally about a yard long.

Yaqona.   Fijian plant, the roots of which are used to make kava.

GLOSSARY OF NAUTICAL TERMS

Aft. Near the stern of a ship.

Bare poles. Describing a ship that has taken down all of its sails in a violent storm.

Batten. A thin strip of wood or other rigid but flexible material which, when inserted into a fitted pocket in a sail, gives shape to the sail.

Beating. Attempting to sail a boat as close as possible to the direction of the oncoming wind.

Beam. The width of a ship at her widest part.

Beam reach. Sailing with the wind on the beam.

Berth. A place where a ship docks or lies alongside a dock.

Binnacle. A stand or housing for the ship's compass placed where it is easily seen from the helm.

Blanket. A point of sail where one sail prevents the wind from hitting another sail.

Block. A case with one or more pulleys mounted on a shaft to gain a mechanical advantage.

Bommie. Slang term for coral head.

Boom. A spar on which the foot of a triangular sail is bent.

Boom crutch. A removable brace fitted into place to support the boom when the sail is lowered.

Bosun's chair. A seat usually made from a board that can be affixed to a halyard and is used to hoist a sailor up the mast to perform work.

Bow. The forward part of a ship.

Bow pulpit. Metal railing surrounding the bow of a ship.

Bridge. An elevated platform on which the wheelhouse and navigation station of a ship are mounted, and where the ship's business is conducted.

Broad reach. Sailing with the wind behind the beam.

Bulkhead. A partition or wall separating areas below the deck of a ship.

Chain plate. A steel plate or bar by which standing rigging is attached to the hull.

Close hauled. Sailing as close to the direction of the oncoming wind as possible. See "Beating."

Close reach. Sailing with the wind on the bow, but not close hauled.

Coral head. Growth of coral extending upward from the bottom of a body of salt water.

Cyclone. A very large storm system that rotates around a system of low atmospheric pressure, creating high winds of 74 miles per hour or more and heavy rain. In the northern hemisphere, these storm systems are called hurricanes.

Flying jibe. To unintentionally change tacks by accidentally steering, or being tossed by a wave, away from the wind so that the leach of the sail and the boom swing violently across the eye of the following wind.

Furl. To minimize the size of a sail by neatly rolling or wrapping it and then securing it to a spar with light lashings.

Gale. A strong wind, or more specifically, a wind of 32 to 63 miles per hour.

Genoa. A large foresail that overlaps the mast, offering tremendous power.

Gooseneck. The fitting at the forward end of a boom which connects the boom to the mast.

Gunnel to gunnel. Rolling violently from side to side, or beam to beam.

Halyard. An arrangement of line and blocks employed to hoist a sail, pennant, flag, bosun's chair or dinghy.

Head off. Aim the bow of the boat so that it is further away from the direction of the oncoming wind.

Headstay. A wire cable extending from the mast to the bow of the ship to support the mast.

Heel. The amount of leaning angle of a vessel under sail.

Helm. The wheel, tiller or device controlling the rudder, which is used to steer a ship. The entire apparatus for steering a ship.

Hove to. A means of keeping a ship about 30% off the wind, generally used during storm conditions to effectively stop forward motion.

Hull. The body of a ship between the deck and the keel, exclusive of masts, sails and rigging.

Knot. A speed over the water of one nautical mile per hour.

Knotmeter. An electronic instrument which measures the vessel's speed through the water.

Leech. The trailing edge of a three-sided sail.

Lee shore. A shoreline that lies downwind of a ship's position. The water's edge in the direction toward which the wind is blowing. The term is used to describe a potentially dangerous situation since if the vessel loses control, it will be driven onto that shore.

Leeward. The side of the vessel that is away from the wind.

Line. A rope that is engaged in a specific task on board a ship.

Mainsail. The sail that is attached to the mainmast. In *Dreamer's* case, we had only one mast.

Mainsheet. The line and blocks used to control the angle of the mainsail to the wind.

Mast. A vertical spar on a sailing vessel employed as the support for the sails.

Masthead. The top of the mast.

Mast steps. Steps mounted on the mast that can be used by a crew to climb up the mast.

Morse code. A code consisting of variously spaced dots and dashes or long and short sounds used for transmitting messages by either visual or audible signals.

Nautical mile. The length of one minute of arc of a great circle on the surface of the earth, or 6076.1 feet, whereas a statute mile is 5280 feet.

Painter. A line attached to the bow of a small boat used to tow the boat or to secure it to a dock.

Plane. To power a boat fast enough for the bow to lift clear of the water, allowing the vessel to attain significantly increased speeds.

Port. Referring to the left side of a vessel when seen by someone facing the bow.

Punt. A narrow, flat-bottomed boat, square at both ends.

Radio direction finder. A radio receiver having a directional antenna mounted on a compass card that can be used to take a bearing on charted radio stations. Radio compass.

Reach. To sail with the wind just forward of the beam, or on the beam, or just aft of the beam. All points of sailing except close hauled (beating) or running before the wind.

Rig. Any of the classic combinations of masts and sails.

Running Rigging. All of the wires, blocks, ropes, spars and other hardware installed above deck with which the sails are hoisted and trimmed.

Rudder. A submerged plane mounted astern for steering a vessel.

Scuppers. The openings in the sides of a ship that allow drainage over the side.

Shroud. A permanently installed line or cable that leads from the masthead to chainplates on the hull amidship and which can be made taut to support the mast.

Single sideband radio. A long range radio used for communication.

Sloop. A sailing vessel carrying a single mast mounted slightly forward of the beam.

Spar. The general term for any of the above deck timbers to which sails are bent, such as the masts, booms, gaffs yards and sprits.

Stanchion. A vertical post mounted at the edge of the deck to which cables are attached as a safety measure.

Standing rigging. Wires bracing the fixed spars of a sailboat. Shrouds, forestays and backstays are all part of a sailboat's standing rigging.

Standing waves. A wave that remains in a constant position that can be caused by tide and wind or by an underwater obstruction.

Starboard. The right side of a vessel when seen by someone facing the bow.

Stern. The aftermost part of the hull of a ship.

Stern pulpit. Metal railing surrounding the stern of a ship.

Through hull fitting. A metal fitting secured to a hole through the hull of a boat, usually with a valve attached to keep the fitting in a closed or open position. These fittings are usually used to attach hoses from sinks, toilets and cockpits to drain the fluids to the outside of the boat. *Dreamer* had seven through hull fittings.

Traveler. An arrangement of a wide metal bracket often mounted on the cabin top or deck under the boom to which the sheet block is secured, allowing the sheet block to move to the lee side at each tack.

VHF radio. Short range, very high frequency marine radio used for communication within 25 miles, normally.

Wheel. A spoked wheel on the steering shaft allowing a good purchase and a mechanical advantage, enabling the helmsman to turn and steer the vessel.

Winch. A geared drum turned by a handle to tighten a line attached to a sail. Winches are used to hoist sails and to affect the curvature of the sail.

DEB, ROG and *DREAMER*

VIANI BAY, JACK, SOFI, LOI, THE HOMESTEAD

LAUNDRY and MAY'S 81st BIRTHDAY

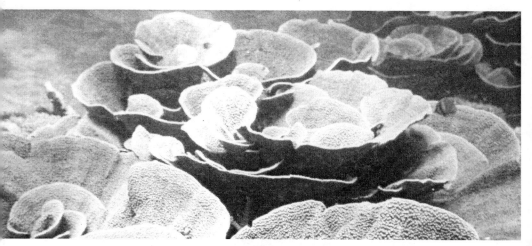

Color is Better Under Water!!

TAMARA, PHIL and JOCKO'S *BURE*

FUN AT BOUMA FALLS

Paul Holmes on the way to the highest falls.

I think our local tourist, Sofi, had a great time at the falls.

Fishing sustains Fijians who are always generous with their catch.

FIJI DAY FINALLY ARRIVES

Young Sara and Pamela.

Vika, Loi and Eroni.

End of Fiji Day.

Rog and I had as much fun as the kids.

INTRODUCING GLORY

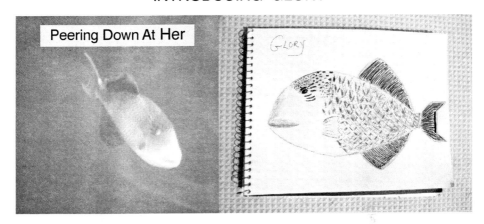

Peering Down At Her

SWIMMING WITH GLORY

After Ed Fisher dies, we hunker down in Matangi Island, using all of our canvas as protection from the heat.

Maku and Qio visit us on *Dreamer*.

Matangi Island Resort

SARA'S 21st BIRTHDAY PARTY

Sara in traditional *Tapa Cloth.*

Sotia and Bob Covert;
Jack and Sofi.

Sara's Mom, Sia Fisher, on the left
and her sister, Eileen, on the right.

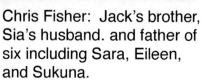

Abu Covert and Andrea Lumkin,
authors of "Ode to Glory".

Chris Fisher: Jack's brother,
Sia's husband. and father of
six including Sara, Eileen,
and Sukuna.

May has her own table with Jack and older brother Bertie in attendance.

After changing into modern clothes, Sara opens her many gifts. First and twenty-first birthdays are the most important.

Back to front: Raua (May's maid), Andrea, unknown on far left, Pamela and Seini.

Young Sara.

Raua, Loi, Sofi, young May, and Andrea
enjoying their Christmas gifts.

We visit Aseta on Yanuyanu Island. In Fijian,
Yanuyanu means island!!

OFF TO SAVUSAVU WITH SOFI AND LOI

SAVUSAVU BAY AND MOUNTAINS
TO CLIMB

RAVIRAVI VILLAGE

Sofi's friends peer into the wet jeep at us.

The ever present children LOVED to play and dance.

Auntie on the left.
Does Sofi look happy or
WHAT!

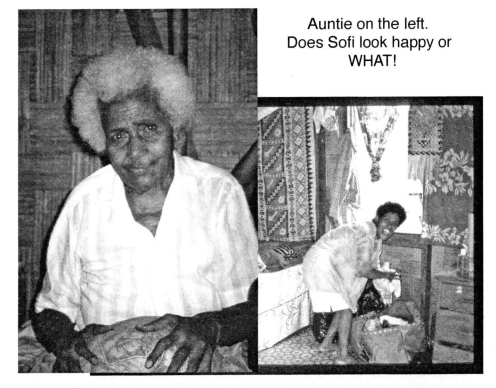

The house is constantly full of visitors.

Sofi and her second daughter, Luciana Divamaiwai.

Debby with Sofi's friend,
Alani Seniceva.

Junior.

ONE LAST ROUND

Jean-Michel Cousteau Resort

Curly Carswell

SAVUSAVU

Ruth and Buddy add more
spice to our lives.

Alex, Ella, Siga, Filipe and John Mitchell. We lost John
to cancer a few years back.

Glory swimming back and forth, back and forth,
back and forth the morning we left.

Memories to last a lifetime .... or more!